SCOTT CONARD, MD

THE SEVEN HEALERS

SIMPLE BUT POWERFUL WISDOM FOR
AN EXTRAORDINARY LIFE

www.rapha7ven.com

Rapha7ven
PO BOX 720999
Dallas, TX 75372-0999
U.S.A.

10 9 8 7 6 5 4 3 2 1
First Edition

This book may be purchased for educational, business, or sales promotional use. For information, please visit www.rapha7ven.com

Designed by Gelson Rocha
Cover photography by Jill Rasco

Library of Congress Cataloging-In-Publication Data is available upon request.

ISBN-13: 978-0-9828048-0-3

contents
THE SEVEN HEALERS

acknowledgments

This book is dedicated to the amazing doctors and staff of TienaHealth whose commitment and caring for their patients continue to inspire me daily.

Dr. Dan Canchola, with his special training and experience in diabetes and urgent care brings consistent, quality care his patients know they can depend on.

Dr. Scott Freeman, a rock of TienaHealth and instrumental in the vision and consistent excellence we strive to achieve in our practice.

Dr. Dar Griffith, whose excellence in every aspect of his life and tremendous experience in musculo-skeletal and physical medicine has him changing lives of people who thought they would never be able to enjoy physical activity again.

Dr. C. Shane Hall, who has expanded the TienaHealth name into the North Dallas area bringing quality care to our Senior Stars.

Dr. Pardeep Shori, whose commitment to teaching and to bringing technology and convenience to our practice is opening new, exciting opportunities for patients and providers.

Dr. David Slater, whose passion and commitment to convenient, timely, preventive, safe care for his patients challenges and motivates our entire team to follow his lead.

Michael Sullivan, PA, whose knowledge of hormonal balance and functioning for both men and women is unparalleled.

Dr. Tearani Williams, whose excellence in woman's health, medical education and her broad experience make her the doctor's doctor when a challenging case is found.

And from the beginning, Dr. Brazos Minshew, an original member of TienaHealth whose commitment to bringing the medical arts of the east and west together to empower clinicians and patients to correct their lifestyles and nutritional deficiencies so they can build health while identifying and ameliorating disease.

introduction
THE SEVEN HEALERS

Living a healthy, fulfilling life is the desire and dream of most if not all people. More than likely it's your desire too and your reason for selecting this book. Being healthy is not just a measure of our physical condition. It is also a measure and reflection of our beliefs, values, and habits that shape every area of our lives. Indeed, what we look like from the neck down is a direct reflection of what has been going on from the neck up.

Now, you may be thinking, *Just what are the Seven Healers, and what makes this book any different than the countless other books available on health?* Good questions. The Seven Healers are seven specific ingredients that every human being needs in order to survive and thrive in this life. These essentials are not limited by a person's nationality, skin color, or religion. They are universally required by all.

The Seven Healers, in order of their necessity for survival, are *Air, Water, Sleep, Food, Play, Relationships,* and *Purpose.* Without these time-tested elements, you cannot flourish and live a meaningful life. Think about it...

* * * * * *

You can only live a few minutes without *air.*

You can only live a few days without *water.*

After about a week with no *sleep*, you will go insane.

You can only live a couple of months without *food.*

Without *play*, which is movement and exercise, you will become sick, miserable, and depressed; within a few months to years, this too would result in death.

Although you can live a lifetime without loving *relationships*, your existence will be shortened and absent of fulfillment.

Likewise, you can live a lifetime without *purpose*, but it will be a life that is incomplete and void of meaning.

* * * * * *

I truly believe many disorders and dis-eases result from an imbalance in or a lack of one or more of the Seven Healers. When this happens, we could say, "What do I need to do to fix this?" Or we could ask ourselves, "*Why am I feeling this dis-ease?*" Finding the root cause of our problem is not so much about asking someone else to tell us what's going on or why we are feeling the way we are feeling. It is really more about looking inside of ourselves and asking, "*What things am I doing on a daily basis that are creating these symptoms? How are these Seven Healers working inside of me? Is one of them lacking or out of balance?*" Once you identify the problem, you can trace it back to the root cause and find the answer, and that is what *The Seven Healers* is all about.

Now, when you envision these Healers, don't see them in a straight line one after the other. Instead, picture them arranged in a circle that has no end. That is, the way you get in touch with your *purpose*, which is Healer #7, starts with *air*, which is Healer #1. All of the Healers are vital, all are interrelated, and none can be neglected.

THE SEVEN HEALERS

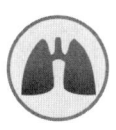 RAPHA**ONE** | AIR

 RAPHA**TWO** | WATER

 RAPHA**THREE** | SLEEP

 RAPHA**FOUR** | FOOD

 RAPHA**FIVE** | PLAY

 RAPHA**SIX** | RELATIONSHIPS

 RAPHA**SEVEN** | PURPOSE

how do you apply the seven healers

Your body is miraculous. Every day your body receives specific "input" you choose for yourself, and from this input, it generates certain results, or "outputs." Everything you put into your body is going to produce specific results. The Seven Healers are vital forms of *input* for your body, and the *output* that results is the quality of the life you live. Incredibly, we did not even need to ask for this— our body came all set up to always take the input we provide it and give us the best results it can.

This book you are holding is not the "gospel" for your body. In other words, it is not the absolute word-for-word truth describing what your body needs to function at optimum health. Actually, it is our *body* that is the "gospel." Only by studying your individual body will you discern the habits with which your body does its best. Since each person's body is unique, not everyone responds to the same input in the same way. If we look at the results and we don't like what we see, we cannot change the truth, or gospel, of our nature—we cannot change the way we are wired to work. What we *can* change, however, is the input, and these Seven Healers are prime ingredients to examine and begin making adjustments.

Start incorporating each of the Seven Healers into your life and give your body time to respond. As you approach your body with these life-giving essentials, you are "asking, seeking, and knocking" at its door to see how it responds. As you do, trust the wisdom of your body. You are fearfully and wonderfully made! Your body's response to the Seven Healers will help you define the "truth" of how you can live a vital and exciting life. That is, how much air, water, and sleep are best for you; which foods and forms of play provide you with optimum health; and which relationships enhance the quality of your life and enable you to fulfill your purpose. You will actually create your own specific recipe for success.

If you get the healthy results you are looking for, wonderful! Keep doing what you are doing. If not, don't quit or get angry with yourself. While it may be human nature, judging and criticizing yourself will only hinder your progress. It may be that what you are doing isn't related to the symptoms you are dealing with, or it isn't enough to achieve the change in your body you would like to see. Try going back and changing the way you are incorporating each of the Seven Healers until you get the results you desire. You may want to talk to your doctor and other professionals who are experienced in the area of health you are having issues with to see how you can do things differently. It is amazing how tweaking things here and there can have a profound effect on our overall health.

change starts with knowing what you want to *be*

Many people attempt to bring change to their lives by first attempting to DO something to make it happen. They think that if they start DOING something different, then they will eventually HAVE what they are looking for and consequently, BE a different person. But the truth is, it doesn't work that way. On the contrary, the person we desire to BE will direct what we DO and consequently, affect the quality of life we HAVE.

For instance, let's say you read about the third Healer, sleep, and you realize how important it is. The first thing that happens on the road to change is you begin to think differently. You say to yourself, *"Okay, that's what I want to BE— a person who gets enough rest."* Well, in order to BE a person who gets enough rest, you are going to have to DO something, which is get in bed at an earlier hour. This may mean going to bed at 10 o'clock and missing your favorite program in order to be able to get up for work at 6 a.m. Initially, you may think, *"That is not acceptable."* But because your desire to BE a person who gets enough rest is stronger than your desire to stay up late and watch your favorite program, you DO what you need to do in order to have what you want to have. DOING, or the action, is the bridge connecting what you want to BE and what you actually HAVE.

All change starts with a choice—a choice to live your life in a certain way. The Seven Healers point to areas you can examine in your life to see if you are living in a way that is consistent with your goals of who you want to BE. If you are committed to BEING a person who has healthy blood pressure, healthy blood sugar, and low cholesterol, you are going to have to DO certain things. Similarly, if you are committed to BEING a person who eats healthy foods, exercises regularly, and is full of energy, there is a certain way you are going to have to incorporate the Seven Healers in order to HAVE that quality of life. Again, what you DO comes from your commitment to BE a certain way.

a final thought before you start

It's been said that the best defense is a strong offense, and this holds true for our bodies too. The Seven Healers are seven specific "players" you have on your team. Through trial and error, you can grow to understand them and "coach" them so that you develop the winning strategy, at your personal age and situation, to live the vibrant, healthy life you desire.

I encourage you to keep an open mind as you read and apply these principles, and don't give up if you don't see instant results. Remember, this is a lifelong *process*. Although it is a challenge, when we get honest with ourselves and take personal responsibility for ourselves, we will start to see changes in our lives. The bad news is that only *you* can make the changes. Thus each of us is responsible for where we are and where we go from here, but that's also the good news. Why? Because *you* control what happens—you can implement changes to bring about healing in your life.

If your health is failing and you keep doing what you have been doing, you are going to keep getting the same results you have gotten. Consequently, you are setting yourself up for discouragement, despair, hopelessness, and ultimately failure. Be open-minded and willing to do new things or old things in a new way. As the ancient book of Proverbs declares,

> **"The intelligent man is always open to new ideas.**
> **In fact, he looks for them."**
> Proverbs 18:15 TLB

As I often say to my patients: You are whole, perfect, and complete *right now*—right where you are. You have everything you need for success. Yes, there are things to overcome, you may weigh more than you want or have high blood pressure, diabetes, or another dis-ease that is frustrating you. But at the end of the day, it will be you in the same body you are in right now, experiencing yourself in a new and wonderful way. You will begin to discover this in your life as you pull the Seven Healers toward you. Your body has all that it needs, so trust its wisdom. It will show you what works best to give you the results you are looking for. Are you ready? Then let's begin our journey. Once you discover the specific combination of things your body needs, you will unlock the door to the healthy life you were meant to live!

"Breathing is so simple—and free! People can't believe it works as a healing and preventative tool"

Herbert Benson, MD[1]

RAPHAONE AIR

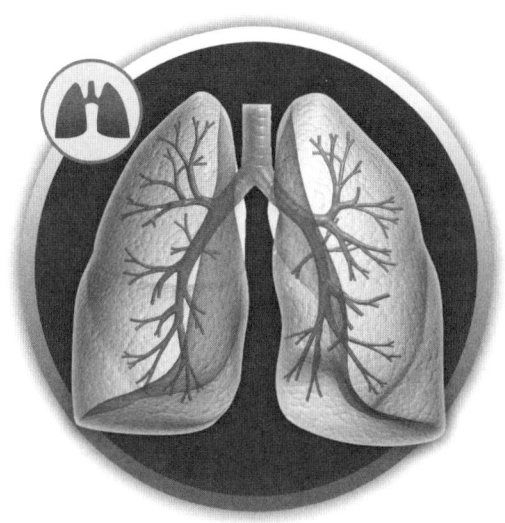

You can only live minutes without *air*.

The first of the Seven Healers is *Air*. Air carries oxygen, a necessary component in energy production to every cell in our body. The act of breathing creates the mechanism that draws vital fluids back into our core for circulation and detoxification. Without breathing, the oxygen sensitive brain cells begin dying in only three minutes. However, with three minutes of deep breathing, your body's stress hormone balance and calm can be restored.

With this central importance, it is not surprising that in Genesis 2 Moses writes,

"And the Lord God formed man of the dust of the ground, and *breathed* into his nostrils the *breath of life*; and man became a living being."
Genesis 2:7 NKJV

Billions of people breathe in and out all day and all night, yet few of us realize just how amazing and indispensable this precious healer is. Let's take a look at some of the basic mechanics of breathing and see how we can better benefit from its healing properties.

what are some of the benefits of breathing?

Respiration, or gas exchange, occurs in our lungs. Did you know that for the first two years after we are born, our infant body actually makes new lung tissue, and after that, the rate of new lung tissue decreases dramatically or ceases? In fact, once we have reached this peak for the remainder of our life we progressively lose lung cells. The rate of this loss is affected by the *quality* of the air we breathe and the *way* we breathe. Theoretically, if we live long enough, all of us will run out of lung tissue. But this will usually not happen until we are very old, possibly well over 100. With consistent damage from toxins like cigarette smoking, asthma, and air pollution this may be accelerated. It is not uncommon for me to see patients with emphysema who are in their forties.

We all think of our lungs as the way we bring oxygen into our bodies. That is not the only role of the lungs and of the act of breathing. Our lungs also function to breathe *out* a byproduct of our cells – carbon dioxide.

How is this accomplished? All of our body's cells reside on a canal system. Not unlike the canal system in the city of Venice Italy the food (and oxygen) comes to the homes and businesses (like the cells in our body) via the canal system. Then the waste from the cells is dumped back into the canal system where it is taken away for disposal. In our bodies the flow goes from the heart (the pump) to the arteries (the largest "waterways"), to the capillaries (small canals) to the interstitial fluid (much less active water around the cells) and then into the veinules, veins and back to the core of the body to be purified and recharged with oxygen and energy. Amazingly, our blood circulates through our body in 23 ½ seconds, feeding and cleansing every cell. And this motion is helped along by the continual process of breathing!

Our body's cells are also adjacent to a second drainage system known as the *lymphatic system*. While our arteries and veins are like the "roads" that run through our neighborhood, the lymphatic system is like the "sewage" system that detoxifies and washes our tissues, removing larger wastes. When we take a deep breath, the negative pressure (suction) created by the expansion of the diaphragm pulls lymphatic fluid from all areas of the body back into our lungs. Once this waste fluid returns to the chest, it then drains into the venous system, which carries the waste and toxins to the kidneys, liver, spleen, and lungs where they are removed from the body. Therefore, not only does breathing assist the circulation system, it also creates the vacuum that moves fluid through the lymphatic system. Truly, we are fearfully and wonderfully made!

how is your breathing?

Now, just because we are breathing doesn't mean we are getting the most from our breathing. As strange as it may sound, there is a more healthy and a less healthy way to breathe. Quick, shallow breaths are less effective: slow, deep breaths more effective for the movement of oxygen, carbon dioxide and fluids around our body.

Many people go through life breathing quick, shallow breaths—they only use a small portion of their lungs' capacity. This is "survival mode" breathing. Actually, we can perform most of life's activities using only 20 to 30 percent of our lungs. This kind of breathing merely inflates the upper chest area but fails to fill the lower airways of the lungs near the diaphragm. Oftentimes, fast-paced, shallow breathing is the result of a fast-paced life and is associated with a decreased ability to concentrate and increased stress in the body.

To understand how fast, shallow breaths affect the body, we need to understand the function of the diaphragm. The diaphragm is a large, domed muscle located between the chest and the abdomen that flexes to pull air in, and relaxes to allow air out of our lungs. To help patients understand how the diaphragm is related to our "stress levels," I teach them about the two adrenal glands located directly under the diaphragm that "monitor" its action. When a person's breathing is fast and superficial, their diaphragm moves up and down rapidly. If these adrenal glands could speak to each other, you can just imagine them saying to each other, "*Oh my gosh! We must be in danger, the diaphragm is racing. Release the stress hormones! Discharge adrenaline, noradrenalin and the cortisol into the blood stream. Bad things are about to happen, and we need as much power as possible to get out of trouble.*" Once stress hormones are released, the body goes into a "fight or flight" mode, which increases the heart rate and blood pressure and creates an overall feeling of mental and emotional hyper-arousal.

I have seen many people, particularly young people, who are really struggling with anxiety and stress. When I was in college, I dealt with stress myself. In fact, I remember one time when I was so stressed out while studying for exams that I went to the emergency room because I felt as if I couldn't breathe. I tried to take a deep breath, but I couldn't seem to get in enough air. I felt as if I was being suffocated or choked. Additionally, my heart rate had risen to about 100 beats per minute. I was afraid.

To my amazement, the medics checked me out and said everything was fine. They determined that my inability to breathe was all a result of anxiety. The problem was not a physical, heart/lung issue—it was mental and emotional.

After this experience, I had other times when I started feeling short of breath. Immediately, I would check my pulse while at rest, it was less than 100 beats a minute, so I knew it was anxiety, not lung or heart disease. To deal with it, I learned to acknowledge it as anxiety and then take long, slow deep breaths to calm myself down. Within a few minutes, the feelings would pass.

This was back in the 1980's when we were just discovering the relationship between our minds, bodies and stress. In the summer between my first and second years of medical school I went to Boston where I was able to attend medical conferences at the famous teaching hospitals associated with Harvard Medical School. At one of these conferences I heard Herbert Benson, MD a cardiologist who was investigating this connection. Soon thereafter he published a book called <u>The Relaxation Response</u> and several research papers which show beyond a shadow of a doubt the relationship between our breathing, the stress we feel in our body, and our health. In addition he and the other researchers at the Benson-Henry Institute for Mind Body Medicine have investigated the beneficial link between the relaxation response and blood pressure, our immune system, pain management, neurodegenerative diseases (like Alzheimer's disease), anxiety, heart attacks, and irritable bowel syndrome just to name a few.

what else affects your breathing?

The other more obvious cause for toxic breathing is inhaling air that has contaminants in it. Being around smoke in any form—whether it is from car exhaust, factory burn off, tobacco smoking, etc.— is definitely a health hazard. The more a person is exposed to airborne pollutants, such as smoking or secondhand smoke, the more accelerated their loss of lung tissue will be.

A study done on women who lived with men who smoked showed that they lived up to *fifteen* years **less** than those who lived with nonsmokers. Clearly, breathing in toxic air damages the lung tissue. It also increases the likelihood of developing respiratory diseases, like asthma, emphysema, and COPD. In addition, just as in their smoking husbands, these studies found that the rate of heart attacks and strokes in these women were significantly increased. The well known association between smoking, heart attacks and strokes is true not only for the smoker but for their wives who lived with them.

In addition keep in mind that our lungs are like "waste baskets" for everything that drains down into them from our upper airways and sinuses. If you have allergies to things, such as pollen, pet dander, dust mites or something else, resulting in a constant drip of mucous down into your lungs, don't ignore this issue. Rinse out your nose regularly with warm salt water and work with your doctor to do what you can to get your allergies under control.

How do our lungs get rid of mucous? The mucociliary transport system has fine hair-like appendages called villi that transport contaminants and mucous up the windpipe and then dump it in the back of our throat where we swallow it and it enters the digestive system.

how can you maximize the function of your lungs?

One of the best things you can do is to *become aware of your breathing*. Being aware of your breathing will enable you to recognize when it becomes fast-paced and shallow. If you are anxious or afraid, and you are aware of it, you can purposely slow down and deepen your breaths. This will significantly impact your body chemistry. Combined with releasing your preoccupation with thinking as outlined below in the Relaxation Response this will increase overall level of peace. It will bring you into a calmer, more stable place from which to live life.

The other thing I would strongly encourage you to do is to *begin practicing deep-breathing*. Deep breathing is really simple and can be practiced in your car, at your desk, or anywhere you go. All you need to do is calmly breathe in through your nose, allowing the air to fill the lower part of your lungs first and then the chest area. Then exhale slowly to the count of five through your mouth. To confirm you are taking full, deep breaths place one hand on your stomach and the other on your chest and breathe. If the hand on your stomach moves for the first two to three seconds of your breath, you're getting a deep effective breath.

One study shows that women who were overweight who practiced ten minutes of deep breathing in the evenings saw a significant *decrease* in their weight. It is believed that the reason for these results was the decrease in the release of stress hormones—specifically cortisol, which has been directly linked to weight gain. Deep breathing also helped these women sleep better at night.

As you begin practicing deep breathing, you may find yourself coughing a bit or even coughing up mucous. If this happens, don't be alarmed; it is actually a good thing. It means the lower portions of your lungs are being expanded, loosening up phlegm in your lower airways. It is not unusual for me to listen to people breathing through my stethoscope and hear a sound like crinkling paper from collapsed lungs re-expanding. Amazingly, after two or three slow, deep breaths, their lungs clear and they sound fine.

Now don't make the mistake of breathing *fast* and deep. This combination leads to hyperventilation (over-breathing). You may find that you are getting dizzy, lightheaded, and developing tingling around your lips and your fingertips. Instead, breathe slow and deep. This will help calm your mind, lower your blood pressure and heart rate, improve your circulation in your hands and feet, and increase your ability to concentrate. By taking deep, slow breaths for a matter of minutes, you can even effectively lower the level of stress hormones in your body by *80 percent*!

So make every effort to incorporate the wisdom of Healer 1 into your life. Slow your breathing and keep the air you breathe as clean as possible. When you sense anxiety coming on you, begin to take slow, deep breaths. Having a strong air system in your body will enable you to fight off bacteria, viruses, and airborne toxins. When you are ready to take it to the next level expand your practice and start doing the Relaxation Response outlined below 1 – 2 times every day. Indeed, learning to be aware of and control your breathing will powerfully impact your life! And the best thing about air is it's **free**!

The basic steps for performing the Relaxation Response

- Pick a focus word, phrase, image, or prayer (The Lord is my shepherd, shalom, peace, and so forth) or on your breath if you prefer,
- Sit quietly in a comfortable position,
- Close your eyes,
- Relax your muscles,
- Breathe slowly and naturally, repeat your focus word as you exhale,
- Assume a passive attitude. Don't worry about how well you are doing. When other thoughts come to mind, quickly say to yourself "oh well," and return to your breathing and repeating your word,
- Continue for 10 to 20 minutes
- Practice this 1 – 2 x/day

From Herbert Benson, Your Maximum Mind

LOCATE YOURSELF

Generally speaking, how would you describe your breathing? Is it working for you? Take an inventory of your environment at home, at work, and the places you frequent. What is the quality of the air you are breathing?

Are you being exposed to pollutants? Can you remove them? What adjustments can you make personally to make the most of this simple yet profound healer?

A QUICK ENCAPSULATION

The first of the Seven Healers is *Air*. You can only live minutes without it. Your body eliminates significant waste and toxins through breathing. While quick, shallow breaths are toxic and are associated with stress in our body, slow deep breaths increase concentration, lower stress hormone levels, and create an environment of peace. Two of the best things you can do to regain the full function of your lungs is to *become aware of your breathing* and *begin practicing deep-breathing exercises.*

YOUR SEVEN HEALERS SCORE

Rate yourself on a 1 – 10 scale: 1 – Never, 3 – Sometimes, 5 – Half the time, 7 – Mostly, and 10 – Always, on these two statements;

_____ I am aware of my body and take deep breaths to manage my stress.

_____ I put aside time to practice deep breathing (the relaxation response).

Go to **www.mysevenhealers.com** and get your full Seven Healers Score™

"Every twenty-four hours, the body recycles the equivalent of forty thousand glasses of water to maintain its normal physiological [body] functions. If you think you are different and your body does not need eight to ten glasses of water each day, you are making a major mistake."

F. Batmanghelidj, M.D.[1]

[Word in brackets added for clarity.]

RAPHATWO WATER

You can only live a few days without *water.*

Water—it is the second of the Seven Healers and is a phenomenal substance that has no equal. It covers over 70 percent of the earth's surface and in our youth makes up **70 percent** of our body. When combined with carbon and other specific elements, it composes nearly all the molecules of living creatures. Indeed, without water, there is no life!

To help us understand the importance of water in our lives, we have to put it in the proper perspective. Just as we live our lives in air, water is the "medium" in which we operate—our bodies live submerged in water. Once air enters our lungs, oxygen flows into the blood. Another way we could say this is that the oxygen "dives into the water-based fluids of our bodies." The same thing occurs when we swallow and the food and water pass across the lining of the gut. We could say that our food and water "dive into the water-based fluids of our bodies." In a sense, all of us are just bags of water walking around in air!

The amount of water in our bodies represents a balance between the amount of water we drink and the amount that evaporates, or is cleared, from our body by the kidneys and intestines. The way water is spread throughout the body is in a well-defined pattern across several "spaces" within. Approximately 66 percent of the water is found *within* our cells, whereas 33 percent is found *outside* our cells. Only 25 percent of this fluid, or 8 percent of our total body water, resides within the blood vessels in our body.

Interestingly, one doesn't have to go far in the Holy Scriptures to find the mention of water. Within the first fifty words, before the second verse of Genesis 1 is completed, water appears on the scene. It was there at the foundation of creation. In fact, God Himself is called the *Fountain of Living Water*, and all who come to Him will be quenched of their thirst.[2]

Water is absolutely essential in liquid form for all the key processes of life, including circulation, respiration, digestion, excretion, and reproduction. Without a fresh flow of this liquid life entering your body and replenishing your cells every day, your body's ability to function will decline. The fluids in your body will become stagnant, and stagnation is a breeding ground for physiologic (internal) stress and disease.

If you were to fly over the state of Florida, you would notice the ground is covered with numerous "potholes" of water. Literally hundreds of ponds cover the state. Many of these have no inlet or outlet of fresh water; they are stagnant. Over time, algae and other oxygen-consuming organisms begin to grow, depriving the ponds of oxygen and nutrients. Fish begin to die and eventually a swamp-like environment often filled with mosquito larvae and bacteria begins to flourish.

The key to cleansing and maintaining the vitality of these "bodies" of water is to establish a continuous movement of water. Similarly, to avoid becoming stagnant and contaminated like these ponds, we can make sure we are drinking adequate amounts of water every day. Let's look at some of the amazing benefits of taking in fresh, clean water, the problems that result when we are dehydrated, and how to ensure that we are getting enough water for our personal shape and size.

one of water's greatest roles

In addition to *providing a foundational building block within* our cells, water fills the canal system of our body, providing the mechanism for detoxifying and cleansing it. As we learned previously, each of our cells are like houses residing on these canals, bathed in fluid (interstitial fluid) that flows into larger blood vessels and the lymphatic "drainage" channels for further detoxifying.

As these houses (cells) perform their daily activities, they run their microscopic engines by taking in oxygen and energy (fats and carbohydrates), and create waste or toxins (such as lactic acid and carbon dioxide).

Once these toxins are generated, our cells dump them into the "pools" of water around them. The fluids of our bodies (all based in water) then rinse out the cell and the surrounding tissue, carrying toxins away into the blood stream and lymphatic system. The fluid eventually travels to the spleen, kidneys, liver and the lungs where it is filtered and toxins are detoxified or eliminated from the body.

When we maintain our bodies with a generous supply of water, our cells and the channels of our lymphatic system flow vigorously, rinsing the body of toxins. If we don't take in adequate amounts of water, we become volume depleted or dehydrated (without—de; water—hydra) and these toxins begin to build up inside of us. Instead of washing toxins out and eliminating them, we end up recirculating them within our body. It is not hard to imagine these toxins building up like sludge in ponds, gradually gumming up our system and/or washing into other tissues, injuring cells and leading to chronic pain and irritation.

As an example, think of your bloodstream and lymphatic system as a mountain stream. If the mountain stream is full of water, you could throw a basketball in at the top of the mountain, and it will eventually be washed all the way to the end of the stream. On the other hand, what would happen if you threw a basketball in a stream experiencing a drought and it had been reduced to just a trickle? Yep, you guessed it—it would more than likely get stuck just a few feet from where it went in and never make it downstream.

To a great degree, this is what happens in our body when we are *under hydrated* or *dehydrated*. The basketball represents toxins that don't belong in us and need to be washed out of our body. If there isn't enough water to effectively carry them through our system and out of the body, they will begin to collect and cause problems. Toxins will actually be washed out of one cell, only to end up getting stuck in another. Once trapped, they can accumulate in muscle tissue, joint cells, etc., causing the area to become inflamed, sore, and painful. This would manifest in our body as muscle aches, joint pain, headaches, fatigue, and soreness. These are all signs of not having enough water flowing through your body.

don't wait till you're thirsty to drink

Interestingly, when we are born, our infant bodies are over 80 percent water. By the time we die, we have often decreased to 50 percent or less water in our bodies. This change is aggravated and accelerated by a decrease in our sensitivity to the need for water that occurs as we age. As soon as babies become 5 percent volume depleted, everybody knows it—they become irritable and cry until they are given a drink or fed. In contrast, a ninety-year-old person can become 10 – 20 percent dehydrated for several days without even feeling thirsty enough to replenish their volume.

Several years ago I was working in a nursing home taking care of patients. One pattern that surprised me was seeing people who appeared to be doing very well one day having to be rushed to the emergency room after only a few days to a week later, virtually in a coma. Given my status as the primary care doctor, the ER staff would call and report, "Dr. Conard, you saw Mrs. Williams (a fictitious name) a short time ago... She was fine until three or four days ago when she became less responsive and began going downhill. She then began to spend more time in bed and her oral intake decreased."

After running some basic blood tests and looking over the results, the problem appeared—Mrs. Williams was dehydrated and had a urinary tract infection. Her sodium level was significantly elevated, and she was dehydrated. Immediately, in the ER, her IV was increased to increase the fluids pumping into her body. Before long, Mrs Williams perked up, and within about six hours she was much better and on her way to her hospital bed or back to the nursing home.

Again, as we age, we lose our sensitivity to thirst and can become more and more volume depleted or dehydrated before we become thirsty. My point is, don't wait until you are thirsty to drink. Keep yourself hydrated, and you'll keep yourself out of a lot of trouble.

when something is wrong in our body

Often we know something is out of balance in our body, but we don't go looking for the exact cause of the problem. Unfortunately, many people translate not feeling good with, "I'm hungry," but that is not necessarily the case. It may be that we are breathing too shallow or too fast and we need to take some deep breaths. It may be that we need more sleep. Or it may be that we need to take in more water.

I frequently see patients with chronic muscle aches in their upper back, neck, and shoulders. For some, these symptoms have been diagnosed by another physician as fibromyalgia or muscle-trigger-points. A second common problem I see is people who say they are constantly feeling tired, sluggish, or head-achy. In both cases, the first step is to have the patient begin to increase their intake of water as well as their number of hours of sleep.

For many who are suffering with muscle aches, this helps significantly reduce or alleviate the pain within a short time. Similarly, many of those feeling sluggish or suffering from headaches also see improvement—they begin to feel sharper and more awake. Often these symptoms are the result of higher concentrations of toxins building up as well as the effect of volume depletion or dehydration of the brain cells. If brain cells, which are very high in water content (some estimate up to 85 percent) are bathed in toxins and lacking the necessary water to function, it is not surprising that they become sore and irritable. This tends to produce headaches and feelings of fatigue. Amazingly, the cure is often simply to increase water intake!

When our bodies begin to run low on water, where does it search for and extract water? Surprisingly, it is not from our blood as you might expect. The answer is from within and around our body's cells. Over 90 percent of the water that we lose is pulled from our cells and the "pools" of water around them. As water is extracted from our cells and passes to the surrounding pools, they shrink—kind of like a plump, juicy grape that loses its moisture in the sun and turns into a raisin. These pools then drain the water (now called interstitial fluid) to the lymphatic channels and/or into the blood vessels, which work around the clock to eliminate toxins from our body. The longer this drought condition persists, the more likely toxins will accumulate in the body and cause problems.

During this time, there are a variety of symptoms we may experience, including a foggy feeling in our thinking, an inability to concentrate, and a drop in our level of energy, which may feel like our blood sugar is dropping or like we are getting ill. Another common sensation is having cold hands and feet. Lack of water also contributes to constipation in many people. Over time, continual constipation may lead to the development of hemorrhoids. If conditions of dehydration persist, it can lead to *desiccation*, which is a loss of fluid in the discs in our back. For many people, this is the cause of their chronic back pain. As you can see, water is vital to many areas of our body.

The bottom line is, if we are not drinking enough good, clean water, we are not going to regularly eliminate toxins from our body. Consequently, if we are not eliminating toxins, they are recirculating in our system and will eventually affect our tissues, resulting in numerous problems. If you're not feeling well and are experiencing some of these symptoms, your body is trying to tell you something. It may be that you are suffering from a lack of water, and it is trying to tell you to "Drink up!"

answer to common questions

What are "toxins"? While a toxin is often considered a poisonous substance, especially one produced by a living organism, the way we are using the term here primarily means products or byproducts of ordinary bodily activities (metabolism), such as lactic acid, which must be managed before its level builds up and causes symptoms like headaches, muscle aches, and fatigue.

How much water should I drink? One adage that has been passed along by many is to drink eight to ten glasses per day. From a medical research standpoint, the basis for this claim is sketchy at best. Another rule of thumb is to take your weight, divide it in half, and that equals the number of ounces of water you need daily. Again, this is not based on a lot of research. If you are doing either of these and it is working for you, great—keep at it. But my experience has been that for some people, this is still not enough, and for others it is too much. Therefore, I encourage my patients to go straight to the source—their body—and learn to listen to what it is saying. We know that when you have enough water, the color of your urine changes from yellow to clear. So perhaps the best way to know that you are getting enough water is to aim at having "pitch-white" pee all the time.

Keep in mind, when you eat fresh fruits and vegetables, you are taking in water. Most produce is high in water content, such as lettuce, which is over 90 percent. Therefore, if you are eating five to ten servings a day, you could easily take in at least a quart of water.

Could some of my hunger really be because I am thirsty instead? When you feel like snacking, drink a glass of water instead. Years ago when I was trying to lose excess weight, I often experienced a sinking feeling, or overall loss of energy, around two or three o'clock in the afternoon. My first impulse reaction was to grab a candy bar and a coke. But I retrained myself to drink a 16 ounce glass of water first and get up and move around. Many times after I did this, the symptom would resolve and I would feel re-invigorated. I was confusing being volume depleted with hunger!

How can I know I am getting enough? Again, pitch-white, clear pee is the key. The color of your urine indicates the concentration of toxins being expelled from your body. If your urine is brownish yellow or darker, it is full of toxins. The clearer your pee, the more toxin-free! Now, if you have taken vitamins earlier, your urine will be fluorescent yellow, and that's okay. It just means you have expensive pee.

So make a conscious choice to drink plenty of fresh, clean water daily. Steer clear of sodas and other sugary or caffeinated beverages as much as possible. Caffeine is a diuretic, which makes you lose water, and sugar tends to be toxic to your system. Pure fruit and vegetable juices are good, but nothing can take the place of just plain H_2O. As you hydrate your body, your cells will become filled with the liquid of life!

Drinking an Adequate Amount of Water Daily Will ...

- Improve your memory and ability to concentrate.
- Reduce stress, headaches, allergies, and the muscle pain.
- Enhance the health of your heart.
- Make your skin smoother and reduce the effects of aging.
- Boost your immune system and enrich your sleep.

LOCATE YOURSELF

Do you have a river of life flowing through you? About how much water are you drinking daily? What is the usual color or your urine? Are you experiencing any of the common symptoms of dehydration? If so, which ones? After reading about this healer, what adjustments do you feel prompted to make?

A QUICK ENCAPSULATION

Water is Healer #2 and it is absolutely essential for all the key processes of life. In addition to nourishing your cells, water is a major detoxifying and cleansing agent in your body. Without adequate amounts of fresh water daily symptoms such as muscle aches, joint pain, headaches, fatigue, and soreness can begin to appear. Don't wait until you are thirsty to drink. Keep yourself hydrated, and you'll keep yourself out of trouble.

YOUR SEVEN HEALERS SCORE

Rate yourself on a 1 – 10 scale: 1 – Never, 3 – Sometimes, 5 – Half the time, 7 – Mostly, and 10 – Always, on these two statements;

_____ I reach my water drinking goal every day (enough water to make my urine clear or light yellow),

_____ I substitute water for sugared and/or caffeinated beverages.

Recommended Resources: _Your Body's Many Cries for Water_, by Dr. F. Batmanghelidj, M.D.

Go to **www.mysevenhealers.com** and get your full Seven Healers Score™

(1) Jordan S. Rubin, The Great Physician's Rx for Health & Wellness (Nashville, TN: Thomas Nelson, 2005) p. 45.

(2) See Jeremiah 2:13; John 4:10; 7:37,38.

"Several studies have evaluated the long-term health effects of getting regular sleep. The data, drawn from reports from around the world, show that sleeping seven to eight hours a night provides protection against needless aging. ...The next time you think you can skimp on shut-eye, remember that sleep is one of the healthy habits that keep you young. Sleep helps strengthen your immune system, boosts your attention span, and dissipates excess stress that can damage your arteries, stomach, and immune system."

Michael F. Roizen, M.D.[1]

RAPHATHREE SLEEP

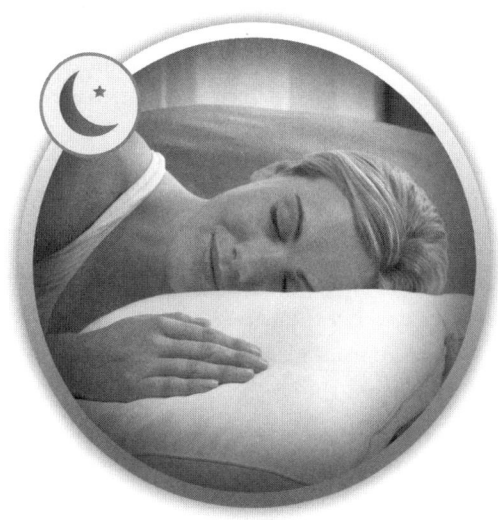

You can only live about a week without *sleep*.

Sleep is an area of utmost importance and is the third Healer worthy of our attention. While air and water detoxify and cleanse us, sleep rebuilds us *physically*, mentally, and emotionally. Unfortunately, as a nation we are largely sleep deprived. While people slept an average of nine hours a night in 1950, today we only get about six to six and a half hours. If you're getting six to six and a half hours of sleep, you may be average, but usually you're not getting the seven and a half to nine hours needed for optimal health.

Many people live their lives in a sleep deprived state, especially single moms and college students. When I was a resident physician in Tampa, Florida, I lived my life on very little sleep. I was on call every third night and was often awake twenty-four to thirty-six hours straight. This definitely had a negative impact on my life—especially my driving. Often after a long shift, on the drive home I would find myself falling asleep and changing lanes or running onto the median. One time during the stop and go traffic of rush hour, I remember pulling up as close as I could to the car in front of me. That way, if I fell asleep I would only gently "bump" them. Actually, it has been found that driving while sleep deprived is just as critical as driving while under the influence of alcohol because it drastically impairs a person's judgment.

Sarah was a twenty-year-old vivacious young woman who lived a very active life in Salt Lake City, Utah. Unfortunately, she was so active that she left very little time in her schedule for sleep. One day she decided to drive to Las Vegas to visit her family and friends. After an enjoyable visit, she headed back home. It was late, but since she had made the trip countless times, she probably thought it was no big deal.

No one knows the exact details, but we do know that 5 ½ hours through the six hour drive she fell asleep at the wheel. Her pickup truck hit the median, frantically, she jerked the wheel trying to correct her course; the truck lurched and then rolled over. In an instant, she was thrown out the window, the truck rolled over her, and her life ended.

What a tragedy, and all from a lack of sleep! We may feel like we can't afford to take time to sleep, but the truth is, we really can't afford not to. Let's take a look at what happens while we sleep, the consequences of being sleep deprived, and what we can do to improve our sleep and, consequently, the quality of our life.

what happens while you sleep?

Contrary to what you may think, sleep is a very active time for the body. It allows your mind to mend and incorporate its new information from the previous day, and it enables your body to heal and repair worn and damaged cells. When you fall asleep, you cycle through specific stages throughout the night called NREM sleep; stage N1, stage N2, and stage N3, followed by stage R, or REM sleep.

NREM STAGE N1: The first stage of sleep is when you are dozing off and are still somewhat aware of your surroundings. This is when you often experience jerkiness, muscle twitches, and sometimes make funny sounds. **Mentally, you can't distinguish when you are going from being awake to stage one sleep.** You can literally be asleep but think you are awake. That's how a person can fall asleep while driving a car, but still think they are awake. Stage one is when you are most easily awakened.

NREM STAGE N2: During this time, the body begins to more fully relax and transition the more reparative stages yet to come. Interestingly, bears spend their time hibernating in N2 sleep. Although it is a restful period for the mind, studies show that getting N2 sleep, without progressing into N3 will leave a person only partially rested.

NREM STAGES N3: This stage is a period of significant repairing and rebuilding for your body. During this time both the mind and the body are completely paralyzed and relaxed. When you are in stage N3 sleep, you are completely unconscious and you have no sense of your environment or time. I explain to patients that during N3 sleep your body goes through a process similar to what office buildings experience at night. The janitorial crew moves in to clean, refresh, and rebuild anything that was worn or torn the day before, so it will be ready for the next day.

For most of you, the height of this activity takes place in the middle of the night between 2 a.m. and 4 a.m. This is when a number of hormones are released throughout your body, including the popular "anti-aging" hormone HGH (Human Growth Hormone). Many people take HGH because they feel younger, their skin looks better, their muscles feel more fit and strong, and their minds operate more nimbly and quickly. And most are paying $1,400 per month to take it. But remember, if you are getting adequate sleep, which increases even more with lots of *play* (the 5th Healer), HGH is being produced and released at night, free of charge by and for your body, enabling it to effectively repair and heal itself.

STAGE R - REM SLEEP: Immediately following stage N3, you enter stage R or REM sleep, which stands for *rapid eye movement*. During this time, your mind is "awake" and your brain waves look very similar to when you are awake, but your body is still completely paralyzed. Consistent with the dreaming you are doing, your eyes are closed and rapidly moving under your eyelids. It is a common misperception that stage R sleep is our most restful time, but that is not the case – the brain is quite active while dreaming.

What is the significance of stage R sleep? As best we can determine, this is the stage during which the information and experiences from the previous day that have been stored in your short-term memory are integrated into your long-term memory. It is like the RAM memory of a computer being saved and integrated onto the hard drive, storing the information and memories for the long term, allowing the new experiences and information to be compared and incorporated with the old.

STAGE CYCLES NEEDED: It's important to understand that *sleep works in cycles*. When you first fall asleep, you begin at stage one and go through stages N1, N2, N3, and R. You then return to stage N1, and the cycle repeats itself (see figure 1 for an actual sleep study report). It takes about 90 minutes to go through one complete cycle of sleep, and for optimum sleep, we need *five to seven* cycles per night.

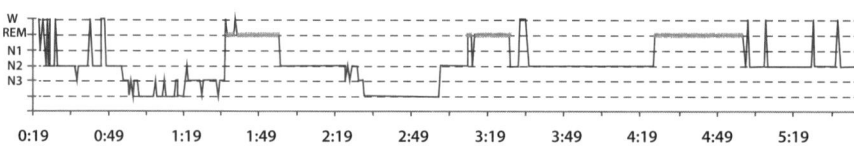

Figure 1. This is an actual tracing from a patient that had a sleep study. You can see that this patient was awake for the first few minutes; she then goes into stage N2 sleep, then N3, then to a period of REM sleep. This is followed by another cycle of N2, N3, and then REM. As the night goes on she has no more N3 but a longer period of REM sleep. You can see she wakes up several times during the night but only for a few moments. You can see that her sleep was limited to about five and half hours only allowing her to go through 3 cycles of sleep.

> **Did You Know ...** A study revealed that children who get A's go to bed an average of forty-five minutes earlier than those who get C's, D's, and F's. Moreover, they fall asleep twenty-five minutes before the children who get lower grades. Indeed, the amount of sleep a child gets makes a big difference in how they perform in school. More sleep = better grades and study habits.

Early in the night, you spend more time in stages three and four sleep and only a very short time in REM sleep. In the next cycle of sleep, stages three and four are shortened, and your REM sleep is lengthened. By the seventh cycle, stages three and four are extremely short or absent. You may go straight into REM sleep from stage 2, and this time REM lasts a long time.

It can be difficult to judge how well we are sleeping during the night. Often we wake up for an instant as we transition from one stage to another (to make sure there are not lions or tigers or bears, oh my!). In addition, we may have environmental light or noise that pulls us into momentary awareness, not to mention the need to get up and go to the restroom or check on the kids. It was a surprise to me as I learned to interpret sleep studies to find that in almost every study I reviewed, it is not unusual to see someone wake up twenty to forty times a night and for them to consider this perfectly normal sleep.

At the other end of the spectrum, "I did not sleep well at all during the study," is a common chorus I hear. But when I show my patients their sleep studies, they see that they slept over 90 percent or more of the night often they are stunned! Remember, in stages N3 and R our awareness of time is distorted. Several hours may go by and without awareness you have no "record" of it in your mind. So be careful not to tell yourself that you are not sleeping well because you woke up several times at night. Your perception of how much sleep you are getting and what you are actually getting often do not match.

how can you tell if you're sleep deprived ... what are the symptoms?

One of the first things to check to see if you are sleep deprived is to see how long it takes you to fall asleep. If you lie down and fall asleep within five minutes, you are "passing out," strongly suggesting you have a sleep deficit. If it consistently takes you more than fifteen minutes to fall asleep, this indicates the presence of anxiety and an inability to calm and relax your mind. Ideally, you want to be able to fall asleep within five to fifteen minutes. This is considered normal and healthy.

Another test to see if you are getting enough sleep is to note how hard it is for you to stay awake in the afternoon. We have a "diurnal" alertness cycle. This means, when you first wake up in the morning, your brain is activated and turned on. Then there is a dip in your level of brain activity between 2 p.m. and 4 p.m. Around 6 p.m. there is another increase in activity that lasts until about 9 p.m. If you are having a hard time staying awake during the afternoon dip and go and get a coke or a candy bar to stay awake, you may be compensating for sleep deprivation. But if you feel fine during this time period without caffeine or other stimulants, then you know you are getting enough rest.

As far as symptoms go, there are many ailments that can develop as a result of being sleep deprived. Common complaints patients tell me include,

"Dr. Conard, my head, my back, and my neck hurt; I feel fatigued all the time." When I hear this, the first thing I do is see how well they are incorporating the Seven Healers in their life—especially the third one, *sleep*. Almost without fail, I discover that they are only getting five and a half to six hours of sleep per night. Upon hearing this, I turn to them and say, "Based on the amount of sleep you're getting, you are not ill, you are normal. You would actually be abnormal if you didn't feel significant fatigue and soreness. Your body is trying to tell you it needs more sleep to keep going."

When sleep deprivation catches up with us, we often develop illnesses. In addition to muscle aches and fatigue, two of the most common ailments I see related to a lack of sleep are *depression and anxiety*. Don't forget that it is during deep sleep that our body restores the levels of neurotransmitter hormones in our brain. If the hormonal release during sleep stage N3 is disrupted, the proper amount of brain chemicals you produce to make it through the next day becomes out of balance, resulting in agitation and burnout. This is often aggravated because people who are dealing with anxiety generally have trouble falling asleep, and those who are depressed tend to wake up in the early morning hours and are unable to go back to sleep, usually for hours at a time. This is different than waking up for a few minutes to go to the bathroom or reposition yourself and then go back to sleep. Early morning awakening is actually one of the earliest signs of depression and may precede obvious daytime symptoms by six months.

A lack of sleep over an extended period of time also often leads to a *weakened immune system*. Consequently, if a person's immune system is weak, they are more susceptible to infections, such as sinus infections and colds. Adequate sleep empowers our body to be able to fight off infections. Let's say a person walks into a room where rhinovirus, which is the common cold, is present, if they are well rested and following the Seven Healers, their immune system may fight off the infection. However, if they are sleep deprived and are ignoring the wisdom of the Seven Healers, they will more than likely come down with it.

Many other major illnesses are aggravated by sleep deprivation; two examples are fibromyalgia and chronic fatigue. I've had people come in and tell me, "I've been diagnosed with fibromyalgia," but when we look at their sleep patterns, we discover that they are actually sleep deprived. If you think about it, each of us makes an unspoken deal with our body. We say, "Okay, body. If you will hold me up and work and move all day long, I'll lay you down at night and allow you to rest." However, if we renege on our deal to allow our body to rest, when we wake up the next day, it will be compromised. Depriving ourselves of adequate sleep night after night will eventually lead to muscle spasms and pain in our upper neck and back—symptoms found in fibromyalgia. So before a doctor can make the diagnosis of fibromyalgia, it is vital for the patient to be well rested and his or her sleep restored: only then can the physician be sure of the underlying cause.

what's the connection between a lack of sleep and weight gain?

One of the most damaging sleep disorders I've seen is *sleep apnea*. A person with this illness will go to sleep, passing through stages one and two just like anyone else. However, at some point during stages N3 and R, when their muscles are paralyzed and completely relaxed, the tissue of their neck collapses on their breathing tube. This cuts off their air flow and their breathing stops.

In this oxygen-deprived state, they awaken startled and in a panic, causing their adrenal glands to kick in and release stress hormones. Once these stress hormones are released, the rhythm of hormone production needed to repair and rebuild the body is altered. After a quick arousal, often without any memory of it, sleep apnea sufferers will go back to sleep, but because of their condition, many of them remain "stuck" in stage one or two sleep all the time—basically like a bear in hibernation. They get little to no reparative sleep from stages N3 and R, their stress hormone levels remain out of whack, and the chronic stress on their body drives up blood sugar and insulin levels.

Interestingly, most people who can't sleep also can't lose weight. In fact, they tend to *gain* weight, and this is directly connected to sleep apnea. When a person wakes up in a panic and stress hormones are released in their body, it starts an internal chain reaction that causes him or her to gain weight. This is on top of having chronic fatigue and exhaustion. Stress hormones tell fat cells to *hold onto their fat* and *grow*. This means the more chronically sleep deprived and stressed a person is, the more their fat cells are told to grow and the less likely they are to lose weight.

Sleep apnea not only causes weight gain but also premature aging and overall damage to the body. In essence, people with sleep apnea end up stressed out all the time because they are literally being suffocated on and off all night. It is just as if someone were to walk up to you, put their hands around your neck and squeeze it until you suddenly awoke; they would then take their hands off you, allowing you to drift back to sleep momentarily, only to restart the process. To help these patients, we often put them on a CPAP machine, which stands for Continuous

Positive Airway Pressure. This machine keeps their breathing tube open and enables them to receive adequate amounts of stages three, four, and REM sleep.

My dad snored all his life, and as a kid growing up, I thought it was normal. Then when I started learning about sleep and sleep apnea, I asked him to come to Dallas so we could do a sleep study on him. He agreed, and through it we learned that he had sleep apnea and was severely sleep deprived. We promptly put him on a CPAP machine, and he entered REM sleep for the first time, possibly in thirty to forty years! After staying in REM sleep for six straight hours, he woke up and said he could not remember feeling that good in years!

If you have disturbed sleep or think you have sleep apnea, have a sleep study done. If the condition is confirmed, start getting treated for it immediately. It is estimated that for every year a person suffers with significant sleep apnea, their IQ drops 1 percent. Treatments, like a CPAP machine, will enable you to sleep restfully, get your hormones balanced, and create successful long-term weight loss. Ultimately, losing excess weight will enable you to get rid of sleep apnea altogether.

getting adequate sleep can help you ...

Overcome crankiness and irritability · Reduce fatigue during the day · Increase short-term memory · Focus on tasks · Be more motivated · Escape the couch potato syndrome · Think and feel more positive about life · Achieve hormonal balance · Improve thinking, IQ, and performances on tests · Decrease accidents and injuries

how can you get more sleep?

Taking a quick catnap during the day will go a long way. For most people, keeping their nap between ten and thirty minutes is best and about the same amount of time needed for one cycle of sleep. On the weekends, you may want to sleep in late or take an extended siesta of an hour or two in the afternoon.

This is a great way to recharge your body.

People sometimes ask me, "Can I skip sleeping for two or three days and then sleep for twenty-four hours straight?" The answer is no; our bodies don't work that way. You can pick up, or pay back, some sleep debt, but only about two hours at a time. Therefore, the key to getting caught up on your sleep is to add a little extra each night until you feel the difference.

Realize that there are many hormones in your body waiting for their daily "cue" from you that tells them when it is time to get moving. Two of the best cues you can give your body is when you *go to sleep* and *wake up at a fixed time*. The goal is to be consistent within 15 minutes with when you go to bed or get up each night. Having a consistent bedtime or rise time will increase your hormonal balance, reduce fatigue, and improve the overall function of your body.

The next time you feel tired and want to get up to grab a soda, candy bar, or cup of coffee, stop and ask yourself, "Why am I doing this—what is going on in my body that is triggering this action?" As you retrace your steps, you may discover that the root reason you're feeling that way is because you're not getting enough sleep. Caffeinated drinks and sugary snacks may give you a quick boost of energy, but this is temporary and artificial. Take a few deep breaths, get up and move around, drink a big glass of water, and get in bed on time consistently!

Don't let the fast pace of the rat race rob you of your precious sleep. Aim at getting seven and a half to nine hours of sleep a night—that's about **fifty-four (54) hours per week**. This includes catnaps and extended siestas on the weekend. As you commit to adjusting your schedule to maximize your sleep, over time your body begins to heal a multitude of dis-eases that you never would have suspected were tied to this third, and very important Healer.

how much sleep debt do you have?
take the epworth sleep test and see

0 - Never doze **1** - Slight chance of dozing **2** - Moderate chance of dozing **3** - High chance of dozing

Read through and rate these activities from 0 to 3:

_____ Sitting and reading

_____ Watching TV

_____ Sitting inactive in a public place, like a theater or meeting

_____ As a passenger in a car for an hour without a break

_____ Lying down to rest in the afternoon when circumstances permit

_____ Sitting and talking to someone

_____ Sitting quietly after lunch without alcohol

_____ In a car while stopped for a few minutes in traffic

_____ TOTAL

If you scored...

Less than 1 - 6, you are getting enough sleep.

7-8, you score is average.

More than 8 please seek the advice of a medical professional with sleep expertise.

LOCATE YOURSELF

How long does it take you to fall asleep? How do you usually feel in the morning when you wake up—tired or well rested? Do you dream on a regular basis? Do you snore at night? For at least one week, keep a log of how many hours of sleep you get each night; note how it compares with the target amount of fifty-four hours and how you feel physically. What adjustments do you feel you need to make to ensure you get good sleep?

A QUICK ENCAPSULATION

Sleep is Healer #3 and it is vital to every aspect of your life. You need seven and a half to nine hours of sleep a night for optimal health. That's about fifty-four hours per week and includes powernaps and extended siestas on the weekend. When you sleep, you cycle through five specific stages throughout the night: stage one, stage two, stage three, stage four, and stage five, which is called REM sleep. Each stage allows your body and mind to repair and heal itself. With adequate sleep, you can achieve hormonal balance, strengthen your mind and immune system, and reduce fatigue and irritability.

YOUR SEVEN HEALERS SCORE

Rate yourself on a 1 – 10 scale: 1 – Never, 3 – Sometimes, 5 – Half the time, 7 – Mostly, and 10 – Always, on these two statements;

_____ I sleep 54 hours each week.

_____ I am consistent with the time of night that I go to sleep and/or the time of morning that I wake up.

Go to **www.mysevenhealers.com** and get your full Seven Healers Score™ and Sleep Diary to begin following your sleep habits.

Recommended Resource: *The Promise of Sleep* by William C. Dement, M.D., Ph.D.

(1) Michael F. Roizen, Real Age: Are You As Young As You Can Be? (New York, NY, Harper Collins, 1999) pp. 242-244.

(2) See the Bible, Psalm 23:2,3

"The body requires energy for all its functions, from the beating of the heart and the elimination of wastes to the transmission of electrical and chemical signals in the nervous system. It gets its energy from food, by taking it in, digesting it, and metabolizing its components. Food is fuel that contains energy from the sun, originally captured and stored by green plants, then passed along to fruits, seeds, and animals. Humans eat these foods, and burn the fuel they release and capture the stored solar energy. As long as we live, we have to eat and eat often."

Andrew Weil, M.D.[1]

RAPHA**FOUR** FOOD

You can only live a couple of months without *food*.

Food **is the strongest drug we put in our bodies.** What is a drug? By definition, the meaning of the word *drug* is "a chemical substance that affects the processes of the mind or body." It is also defined as "any chemical compound used in the diagnosis, treatment, or prevention of disease."[2] Now, you may be thinking, *How can food affect a person's mind?* Well, think back to the last time you ate a steak and baked potato and a time when you just had a large salad. How did you feel after you had each one? Indeed, there was a marked difference in your level of calmness and energy. My point is, the effects of food are powerful! In fact, most of our early pharmaceutical agents were derived from herbs and other plants, and today one of the fastest growing industries are nutraceuticals—a system of using vitamins, minerals, and herbal products to treat medical conditions. With this perspective it is easy to understand why the food choices we make every day will enhance or diminish the quality and quantity of our lives.

On average, an adult eats about 2,000 calories of food daily, which is 200,000 milligrams of food. Unfortunately for many Americans, their diet is dominated by junk foods, fried foods, and fast foods. These are highly processed, high starch and fat, metabolic blasts that are rich in calories but low in many of the most vital nutrients like vitamins, minerals, and phytonutrients. Can you guess what the three most common foods eaten by Americans today are? White bread (high starch, low in nutrients), coffee (good news—no calories; bad news— few nutrients), and hot dogs (a saturated fat bomb).

Indeed, times have changed since 1900, when Americans ate an average of 5 pounds of sugar per year. In 2000, the amount of sugar consumed rose to 163 pounds! Although our bodies have not evolved or changed, our diet sure has. It is truly amazing, maybe even miraculous, that our bodies have been able to cope with and manage this thirty-fold increase. However, it has not come without a price. While our pancreas produced 5 to 10 units of insulin to process an average meal in 1900, today it is not unusual for me to see blood insulin levels of up to 100 units in a person trying to handle an average meal. The organ that bears the brunt of this drastic change in our diet is our pancreas, which manufactures insulin (and other hormones). Type 2 diabetes occurs when the demand for insulin exceeds our body's ability to produce it. Surprisingly, people with diabetes are often making *ten times more insulin* than people who do not have diabetes. Yet, the demand in their body is over ten times greater, so they have a relative shortage of insulin. This is occurring at record rates today—both in adults and children. To make matters worse, we now recognize that people with elevated blood insulin levels not only are battling diabetes but are also at a greater risk of heart attacks and strokes.

How can we combat these destructive trends? I truly believe it starts with understanding what's going on inside our body during digestion, which is the absorption of energy from the gut, and metabolism, which is the processing of that energy. Once our eyes are open to this amazing process and we can see how different foods affect us in different ways, then we can begin to make wiser food choices and create a recipe for healthy living.

understanding the process of digestion

The digestive process is truly miraculous and it all begins in our mouths. Once our food is thoroughly chewed and mixed with saliva, it moves down the esophagus (swallowing tube) and into the stomach. There, hydrochloric acid begins to zealously break it down and kill any bacteria that may be present. From the stomach, the food passes into the small intestines. As it does, the pancreas, an organ adjacent to the stomach, releases enzymes into the small intestine to help further break down the food. There are many different types of enzymes, including proteases that break down protein, amylase and lactase that break down carbohydrates, and lipases that break down fats. When enzymes enter the small intestines, they begin to attack the food much like sharks attack the carcass of a dead whale. They break it up into smaller and smaller pieces until it's in its simplest form and can move across the gut wall and into the body.

Interestingly, the body breaks down food into only *three* major forms (macronutrients): carbohydrates, fats, and proteins. Carbohydrates are broken down into *simple sugars*—glucose, galactose (from milk), and fructose (from table sugar, fruits and vegetables). These are sources of rapid energy. Fats are broken down into *free fatty acids, and glycerides,* slower forms of energy and the building block for hormones. And protein, which is the universal building block of the body, is broken down into *amino acids.* While carbohydrates can be broken down and enter the bloodstream quickly, fats and proteins digest more slowly and take longer to absorb.

Once these nutrients, along with many other micronutrients (discussed below), enter the bloodstream, they flow up the portal vein to the liver. The liver's job is to detoxify and package our food so that the cells of our body can utilize it. As soon as the liver's work is done, the food flows into the body in the form of complex fat molecules, glucose, and amino acids. Interestingly, on the way to the liver, the blood flows past the pancreas, which releases insulin into the bloodstream *ahead* of the food. Insulin basically acts as a messenger, notifying the cells, "Food is coming! Food is coming! Get ready to eat!" The cells of the body then open their "doors" and begin to welcome in and enjoy the free-floating feast in the blood.

Each of our cells, depending on its type, will absorb different nutrients from the blood. The brain utilizes only glucose for energy. Most tissues are able to utilize both glucose and fats in the form of triglycerides and free fatty acids for energy. One thing that all cells take in, however, is amino acids. These simplified elements of protein are the building blocks used inside each cell.

Now, the fat cells (adiposities) throughout the body serve a very interesting function. They take energy out of the blood in the form of fat and store it until the body needs it again. If the meal we ate was low in energy, our fat cells will probably have to release some of its stored energy in an hour or two. If the meal was high in energy, our fat cells may not have to release any stored energy for several hours or the whole day. And if we continually take in an excess of energy (calories) in our food or too much food over years it may stay in storage to be carried around literally for the rest of our lives.

Vitamins, minerals, and phytonutrients from plants are all *micronutrients,* and they function as co-factors or the "oil" of all of the cells of the body. They themselves are not consumed as energy or used as building blocks. Instead, they are used in the same way our automobiles use oil, transmission fluid, and brake fluid—to lubricate our moving parts. Without them, our body doesn't function well.

Once all our food has been digested and absorbed and delivered to our cells for use or storage, our insulin level drops. As the presence of this messenger diminishes in our system, the pancreas sends out another messenger—the hormone *glucagon*. Glucagon travels throughout the body, telling fat cells "Release some Energy, Release some Energy!" Soon thereafter, our liver releases glucose into the blood and our fat cells release fat (energy) back into the bloodstream to insure that our energy level doesn't drop too low. This ebb and flow of energy and nutrients in the blood occurs each time we eat, and the process of managing it is called *intermediary metabolism*. The balance between our input (the quality and quantity of carbohydrates, fats, and protein we eat) and our output (how much energy we expend every day), is what determines how we feel and look like physically.

seeing your #1 combo in a whole new light

In light of how our body digests and absorbs food, let's take an eye-opening look at what happens in our body when we eat a fast food meal. Imagine you pull up to your favorite burger joint and order a #1 combo, containing a hamburger, large fries, and a Coke. Once you chew and swallow your food, it enters your stomach where hydrochloric acid kills the bacteria or parasites and begins to break down the food. After this, the combo meal moves into the small intestine where the pancreas unleashes its digestive enzymes that act like sharks on the food, breaking it down into its simplest components. Soon the hamburger is broken down into saturated fat, polyunsaturated fat, amino acids and some B vitamins. The French fries are broken down into glucose, saturated and unsaturated fat, and possibly a few B and C vitamins. Lastly, the Coke is reduced to water, caffeine, glucose, fructose (the basic component of table sugar), and a number of preservatives and food colorings. At this point, this metabolic blast is broken down enough to pass into the bloodstream and begin its trip through the body.

The pancreas, which is responsible for monitoring and responding to the energy level in the blood, immediately recognizes the food entering the bloodstream and begins to release insulin and other hormones into the bloodstream to notify and prepare the body's cells to receive the nutrients. Excess sugar and fat must be removed from the blood in order to prevent serious problems from occurring. Very high levels of fat and sugar in the blood can result in things such as delirium, a coma, and even death. Insulin tells the fat cells and liver to take the fat and sugar out of the bloodstream and store it as energy for future use. These cells open their doors, pulling glucose and fat into them for storage.

Now, if our body mass index (BMI), which is a measure of our weight in relation to our height, is below 25 (go to **www.mysevenhealers.com** to calculate your BMI), there is plenty of room in our cells for storing fat and sugar, and this process proceeds without a hitch. However, if our BMI exceeds 25, then our risk of having problems begins to increase. At some point, when a person's BMI is between 25 and 30, fat cells become filled with energy. Quite literally there is "no more room in the inn." If this is our condition when we are eating our #1 combo, the excess energy flowing in our bloodstream will go to our fat cells, knock on the door, but *not* be allowed to enter because there is no room!

Body Mass Index Table

	Normal						Overweight					Obese										Extreme Obesity															
BMI	19	20	21	22	23	24	25	26	27	28	29	30	31	32	33	34	35	36	37	38	39	40	41	42	43	44	45	46	47	48	49	50	51	52	53	54
Height (inches)															Body Weight (pounds)																					
58	91	96	100	105	110	115	119	124	129	134	138	143	148	153	158	162	167	172	177	181	186	191	196	201	205	210	215	220	224	229	234	239	244	248	253	258
59	94	99	104	109	114	119	124	128	133	138	143	148	153	158	163	168	173	178	183	188	193	198	203	208	212	217	222	227	232	237	242	247	252	257	262	267
60	97	102	107	112	118	123	128	133	138	143	148	153	158	163	168	174	179	184	189	194	199	204	209	215	220	225	230	235	240	245	250	255	261	266	271	276
61	100	106	111	116	122	127	132	137	143	148	153	158	164	169	174	180	185	190	195	201	206	211	217	222	227	232	238	243	248	254	259	264	269	275	280	285
62	104	109	115	120	126	131	136	142	147	153	158	164	169	175	180	186	191	196	202	207	213	218	224	229	235	240	246	251	256	262	267	273	278	284	289	295
63	107	113	118	124	130	135	141	146	152	158	163	169	175	180	186	191	197	203	208	214	220	225	231	237	242	248	254	259	265	270	278	282	287	293	299	304
64	110	116	122	128	134	140	145	151	157	163	169	174	180	186	192	197	204	209	215	221	227	232	238	244	250	256	262	267	273	279	285	291	296	302	308	314
65	114	120	126	132	138	144	150	156	162	168	174	180	186	192	198	204	210	216	222	228	234	240	246	252	258	264	270	276	282	288	294	300	306	312	318	324
66	118	124	130	136	142	148	155	161	167	173	179	186	192	198	204	210	216	223	229	235	241	247	253	260	266	272	278	284	291	297	303	309	315	322	328	334
67	121	127	134	140	146	153	159	166	172	178	185	191	198	204	211	217	223	230	236	242	249	255	261	268	274	280	287	293	299	306	312	319	325	331	338	344
68	125	131	138	144	151	158	164	171	177	184	190	197	203	210	216	223	230	236	243	249	256	262	269	276	282	289	295	302	308	315	322	328	335	341	348	354
69	128	135	142	149	155	162	169	176	182	189	196	203	209	216	223	230	236	243	250	257	263	270	277	284	291	297	304	311	318	324	331	338	345	351	358	365
70	132	139	146	153	160	167	174	181	188	195	202	209	216	222	229	236	243	250	257	264	271	278	285	292	299	306	313	320	327	334	341	348	355	362	369	376
71	136	143	150	157	165	172	179	186	193	200	208	215	222	229	236	243	250	257	265	272	279	286	293	301	308	315	322	329	338	343	351	358	365	372	379	386
72	140	147	154	162	169	177	184	191	199	206	213	221	228	235	242	250	258	265	272	279	287	294	302	309	316	324	331	338	346	353	361	368	375	383	390	397
73	144	151	159	166	174	182	189	197	204	212	219	227	235	242	250	257	265	272	280	288	295	302	310	318	325	333	340	348	355	363	371	378	386	393	401	408
74	148	155	163	171	179	186	194	202	210	218	225	233	241	249	256	264	272	280	287	295	303	311	319	326	334	342	350	358	365	373	381	389	396	404	412	420
75	152	160	168	176	184	192	200	208	216	224	232	240	248	256	264	272	279	287	295	303	311	319	327	335	343	351	359	367	375	383	391	399	407	415	423	431
76	156	164	172	180	189	197	205	213	221	230	238	246	254	263	271	279	287	295	304	312	320	328	336	344	353	361	369	377	385	394	402	410	418	426	435	443

Source: Adapted from Clinical Guidelines on the Identification, Evaluation, and Treatment of Overweight and Obesity in Adults: The Evidence Report.

This causes quite a disturbance in our blood. The energy level in the form of fat and sugar starts to rise, and as a result, the pancreas begins to pump out more and more insulin (say from 10 units with a BMI of 25 to 100 units with a BMI of 35). Again, it prods and cajoles the fat cells to open up and let in the excess energy. As the insulin level rises, the fat cells finally respond and, at some point, they remove the excess energy from the blood. Realize that if our BMI remains high or increases and we continue to eat the foods high in excess energy or too much food our condition will worsen. Consequently, our fat cells will become more resistant to insulin's plea, our pancreas will have to work harder, and the cycle of "insulin resistance," also called metabolic syndrome or Syndrome X, goes on and on.

"saturated" fat cells experience problems

Every person is slightly different, but in general three things start to change when our fat cells reach "saturation." One rather obvious consequence of saturated fat cells is the increase in the amount of oils, or fats, in our bloodstream, especially after we eat. If we went to the doctor during this time and had our blood drawn, we would find that we had high LDL (lousy) cholesterol and/or high triglycerides. This is often accompanied by having low HDL (healthy) cholesterol—the kind we need to clean our blood vessels. What's even worse is that when our blood is super-saturated with triglycerides, the LDL molecules flowing through our blood become even smaller and dense, leading to more aggressive and malignant damage to our blood vessels.

Another negative side effect of saturated fat cells is that our pancreas will begin to wear out from its excessive insulin production. At some point, because it is unable to keep up with the demand, this will result in an elevated blood sugar level (greater than 140 mg/dl if you were to check your glucose level with a glucometer or in a lab test) after we eat. If this pattern persists, the elevation in our blood sugar will begin to be present even *before* we eat (greater than 125 mg/dl). In the United States, often within two to five years (which is too long!), this condition will be found and a formal diagnosis of diabetes will be given.

Finally, our blood pressure will start to creep up. Initially, it may not be by very much, but in certain individuals it can be quite dramatic. I have one patient who has figured out that if his weight increases to 214 pounds or more, his blood pressure will dramatically increase (from the 120/80 range to 150/95-100), and he will need to take blood pressure medicine to bring it down. However, if he stays below 214 pounds, he doesn't have to take medicine. He actually has a clear "weight point" at which his fat cells appear to become saturated and his body begins to release destructive hormones!

Now, all of us experience injuries to our blood vessel walls on a regular basis, but if our system is healthy and working well, it is quickly repaired and it takes decades before a significant problem occurs. However, if we have high blood pressure, high blood fat or sugar, we smoke, have deficiencies in vitamins like folate, vitamin B12, or vitamin B6, and/or we are experiencing significant chronic emotional stress, we will increase the number and severity of these injuries. Once the blood vessel walls are injured, the probability that LDL fat will lodge itself in the wall increases. Over time, this buildup of fat, or *plaque*, within our artery walls, can lead to reduce blood flow and eventually a blockage of the artery. This degenerative buildup of plaque is called atherosclerosis.

Over a period of years, as plaque buildup increases, even without blocking the flow of blood it often becomes unstable—much like a pimple on the wall of the blood vessel. Finally, the pimple bursts open into the blood, resulting in a blood clot forming over the site. This interrupts the flow of blood, causing everything downstream to become starved for oxygen and possibly die. If this happens in our brain, we experience *a transient ischemic attack (TIA)* or a *stroke*. If this happens in our heart, we experience a *heart attack*. The relationship of this process with extra energy in the blood (high triglycerides and LDL) coupled with increasing blood sugar (pre-diabetes or metabolic syndrome) explains why 50 percent of the people already have significant heart disease the day they are formally diagnosed with diabetes, and 80 percent of them will eventually die of a stroke or heart attack.

Now you can better understand how regularly eating fast food combos leads to weight gain, high cholesterol, diabetes, high blood pressure, heart attacks, and strokes. To get a pretty good idea of how much plaque has built up on the walls of your heart's arteries, stand up straight and naked in front of a mirror; turn sideways and take another mirror and look at your reflection. If your belly button protrudes past your nose, most assuredly this process is well under way in your body! The plaque in your body resembles the bulge in your belly. The good news is, as you get rid of the gut, you will often get rid of the plaque! By incorporating the wisdom of Healer #4, *Food*, you can begin to reverse the curse of poor eating one choice at a time.

the keys to healthy eating

Okay, so now that you have a more vivid picture of what is going on, let's look at some positive patterns of healthy eating that will put you on the road to success.

Key: Be Aware of the Quantity of the Food You Eat. To make this easy follow what I call the *Hand Signals of Health*. These are fun and easy to remember, especially since you have your hands with you everywhere you go! Hold up your fist—this is the size of your stomach. Let's fill it with the best protein, carbohydrates, and fat we possibly can.

> **First, vegetables** are a free food—you can eat as much of them as you want. Try to get a rainbow of colors in the ones that you eat. Nature packed different nutrients in different color packages so eating a variety is a great idea!
> **Meat** servings the size of the *palm of your hand* and no thicker than a deck of cards provide the amino acid load that most of us will benefit from each meal.
> Finally, **starches**, which include bread, rice, pasta, potatoes, and corn, **no greater than the size of your fist** (all together) will provide you with all the fast-acting carbohydrate energy you need.

This is the size for one meal. Try to eat two or three meals per day along with two to three snacks (see below, for a more comprehensive discussion of The Hand Signals of Health go to **www.mysevenhealers.com**).

Key: Eat Balanced Snacks and Meals Regularly. The second key is to eat *balanced snacks or meals* and to eat within 2 – 3 hours after snacks and 4 – 5 hour after meals. Start your metabolism in the morning by eating within 30 minutes or so of getting out of bed. Since you have gone without food for several hours through the night, the intake of nutrients soon after awaking gets your metabolism ramped up, consuming calories, and moving in the right direction. A dietitian I used to work with, Pam Neff, used to encourage our patients to get things going by eating a breakfast like a *king* followed by a lunch like a *prince*. Next a mid-afternoon snack of 100 to 200 calorie snack (depending on your size) containing protein, carbohydrates, and healthy fat in the afternoon, followed by eating dinner like a *pauper*. Finally if you have followed the Hand Signals of Health and want too, many enjoy a snack later in the evening before you go to bed.

The importance of the mid-afternoon snack as a quick "pick-me-up" cannot be overemphasized. It will help stabilize your blood sugar, reduce cravings and maintain your energy level during the low energy point in the mid-afternoon. It also sets you up for the evening without having to fight the desire to over-eat during the evening.

I strongly suggest you *don't* do the opposite of this and eat little or nothing throughout the day and then eat a huge meal at night before going to bed. Unfortunately, this is the normal eating pattern for many Americans—they snack or don't eat during the day, and then "graze" from 5 p.m. until 10 p.m. This unhealthy habit leads many people to ingest up to 5,000 calories within a short amount of time in the evening, slamming their body metabolically. Think about it. If I handed you a 30-pound weight seven, ten, or twenty times in a day and asked you to do a few reps and then place it on the floor, you could do it. But what would happen if I handed you 600 pounds all at once? You would struggle to handle it. Similarly, depriving your body of nutrients during the day and then consuming a huge meal during the evening has the same effect on your body.

Key: Give Protein a Prominent Place. I strongly recommend including protein with each snack and meal. It is the building block of every part of the body. By consuming the twenty-two amino acids found in protein, especially the eight essential amino acids our body cannot produce on its own, we will keep the body from turning on itself to harvest these amino acids from other tissues, such as our muscles. Additionally, a meal with a healthy protein source will help us feel satisfied longer; reducing the spontaneous snacking and sinking feeling we often have three to four hours after a high carbohydrate meal. Lastly, eating protein stimulates the release glucagon—the hormone that not only helps you digest protein but also stimulates your fat cells to release energy and get smaller while reducing the production of insulin.

If you live a sedentary lifestyle, you want to consume <u>half</u> of your *goal* weight (your weight at a BMI of 25) per day in grams of protein. If you are involved in vigorous physical activity, this increases to 1 gram of protein for each pound of your goal weight each day. This formula will result in 60 to 200 grams of protein for the average adult (to calculate this go to **www.mysevenhealers.com** and put in your information). One additional note is that taking in protein throughout the day and not all at one time also is important.

In my medical practice (at the weight loss clinic called TienaTrim and Fit), one common habit that I find many patients, especially women, make is to eat less than 50 grams of protein per day. They tend to eat a lot of carbohydrates instead (often packaged with high fructose corn syrup). Add this to the highly variable salt intake in processed foods and hormonal changes, and often the scales will vary 5 – 10 pounds up or down in a single month, regardless of having counted and maintained a stable calorie intake – talk about confusing!

If you focus on putting lean protein in your diet at this level you will find that you end up with about 40 to 50 percent of your calories from carbohydrates, 25 to 30 percent from protein, and 25 to 30 percent from fats. The Zone diet, The South Beach diet, DASH diet, and Mediterranean diet all have many ideas for meals that meet these criteria.

Key: Don't Forget the Fiber! Another life-giving tip is to include plenty of fiber in your diet. While the average American consumes about 5 grams a day, we actually do the best with at least 25 to 30 grams. Fiber is a fabulous free food that works wonders in our system. Much of it goes into our mouth, through our intestines, and out our backside without ever going into our blood. It acts like a cluster of tiny brooms, sweeping and cleaning every crack and crevice of our colon. At the same time, it causes the muscles of the intestines to work harder, making them stronger and fit. Additionally, it slows down the absorption of the glucose (sugar) from the intestines, helping to sustain our energy level throughout the day and avoid extreme highs and lows.

The amount of fiber and water you have in your diet also directly influences your ability to eliminate waste. While an adequate amount of water keeps digested food from getting stuck in your gut, an adequate amount of fiber keeps it moving forward through the intestines. I like to call it "Poopology 101." Ideally, a person should have one to two bowel movements a day (not one to three a week!). How do you know if you're getting enough fiber? Easily releasing a smooth, moist, angel-food-cake consistency, foot-long floater in the commode each day says it all. I know talking about this can be a hard, stinky, messy, sticky job; but over time with the right amount of water and fiber, it actually becomes much less malodorous, and somebody's got to do it! Good sources of fiber include raw vegetables and fruit, beans and legumes, basmati or brown rice, as well as whole-grain breads, pasta, and cereals. If getting the fiber in food just won't work with your lifestyle, Benefiber or Metamucil are other options to help you bulk up.

Key: Get the Skinny on Fat. Fats play an important role in helping us feel full and satisfied. Without eating fat, we tend to continually feel hungry. While trans (altered polyunsaturated fats) and saturated fats increase the chance of heart disease and cancer, monounsaturated and most polyunsaturated fats actually reduce the risk of disease. Keep in mind that fats are the material every cell of our body relies on to make healthy membranes and hormones, which allows them to function properly. Indeed, eating healthy fat in moderation is indispensible.

The tricky part of eating fats is monitoring and controlling the calories. In every gram of fat there are **8 calories**, as opposed to have **4 to 5 calories** per gram proteins or carbohydrates. This is the reason that early diet plans were focused on eliminating fats from the diet, a logical strategy that left patients unsatisfied, craving carbohydrates, and bloated. We appreciate now that fats are not bad; they are just caloric and making the quantity eaten important to manage.

Saturated fats are fats that are solid at room temperature. These are found in animal products such as bacon, sausage, hot dogs, processed sandwich meat, and red meat (the more "marbled" it is, the higher the saturated fat). Saturated fats are also found in dairy products like butter, cheese, milk, and eggs. A certain amount (7 percent of your calories or less) of saturated fat will help enhance your immune system and enable your bones to better absorb calcium. Too much saturated fat has a negative effect on the body as the consumption of high-fat food tends to beat up the inside of our blood vessels and lead to less stable cell membranes.

The next type of fats is *polyunsaturated fats*. In their natural form, they are liquid at room temperature and make the membranes of our cells more flexible and stable. Some of them—the omega 3s—have been shown to reduce heart attacks and fatal heart arrhythmias dramatically. The best sources for omega fatty acids are fish and flaxseed. Unroasted or raw pecans, walnuts, and almonds are also good sources.

Polyunsaturated fats can be altered to produce *trans fats*. These include hydrogenated and partially hydrogenated fats found in margarine, corn oil, and many grocery store cookies, cakes, and pastries. The purpose of trans fats is to increase the "shelf life" of foods, making them less likely to spoil. You can discover trans fats by looking at the food label where manufacturers are required to list what is in the food. If you find this, then you are eating a lot of processed and manufactured foods—a trend best to reverse!

Of all the fats available, *monounsaturated fats* have the best effect on your body. They are associated with an increase in HDL (good) cholesterol and decrease LDL (bad) cholesterol. Monounsaturated fats are found in avocados, olives and olive oil, and nuts. If you find yourself wanting a snack in the midafternoon, a handful of nuts and an apple are a great way to satisfy the hunger and give your body a nutritious gift.

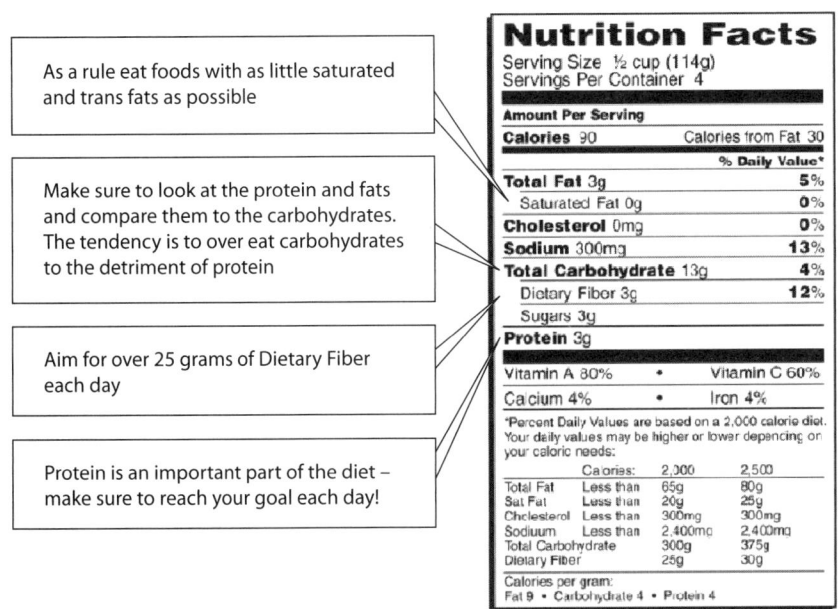

As a rule eat foods with as little saturated and trans fats as possible

Make sure to look at the protein and fats and compare them to the carbohydrates. The tendency is to over eat carbohydrates to the detriment of protein

Aim for over 25 grams of Dietary Fiber each day

Protein is an important part of the diet – make sure to reach your goal each day!

Nutrition Facts

Serving Size ½ cup (114g)
Servings Per Container 4

Amount Per Serving

Calories 90	Calories from Fat 30

	% Daily Value*
Total Fat 3g	**5%**
Saturated Fat 0g	**0%**
Cholesterol 0mg	**0%**
Sodium 300mg	**13%**
Total Carbohydrate 13g	**4%**
Dietary Fiber 3g	**12%**
Sugars 3g	
Protein 3g	

Vitamin A 80%	•	Vitamin C 60%
Calcium 4%	•	Iron 4%

*Percent Daily Values are based on a 2,000 calorie diet. Your daily values may be higher or lower depending on your caloric needs:

		Calories:	2,000	2,500
Total Fat	Less than		65g	80g
Sat Fat	Less than		20g	25g
Cholesterol	Less than		300mg	300mg
Sodium	Less than		2,400mg	2,400mg
Total Carbohydrate			300g	375g
Dietary Fiber			25g	30g

Calories per gram:
Fat 9 • Carbohydrate 4 • Protein 4

Key: Minimize Processed Foods. As a rule, try to eat food as close to its natural state as possible; the longer it spends being processed, transported, and stored, the less likely it is to maintain its nutritional value. I encourage you to eat a wide variety of *living foods* like fresh fruits, vegetables, whole grains, nuts, and legumes. A living food is something that has recently been picked from the vine and is filled with enzymatic activity and nutrients. *Dead foods* are those that are processed or refined. They lose their enzymatic activity and nutrients and should be avoided as much as possible. While hot dogs, bologna, and white bread may taste good and be easy to prepare, they lack sufficient nutrients and will end up causing you more harm than good. As far as meat, choose lean free-range chicken, turkey, and beef. Some widely available healthy fish to consider are salmon or trout. To receive your food's greatest value, eat vegetables raw, steamed, or stir-fried, and meat baked or broiled, not fried.

Living Foods Will Add Years to Your Life and Life to Your Years!

- Soybeans, Beans, Lentils
- Strawberries, Blueberries, Prunes
- Broccoli, Cauliflower, Carrots, Cabbage
- Almonds, Walnuts, Macadamia Nuts
- Parsley, Tomatoes, Garlic
- Pineapple, Tangerines, Grapefruit
- Green Tea, Agave Nectar

The bottom line when it comes to buying food: Spend most of your time shopping the perimeter of the grocery store where all of the freshest foods are found. And by all means, read the label. Look for foods that are high in fiber, protein, monounsaturated fat, vitamins, and minerals. At the same time, steer clear of foods that are high in sugar, sodium, saturated and trans fats. If you can't read the label, don't buy it. If it is packaged, more than likely it is filled with chemicals and preservatives and has little to no nutritional value.

Remember you are as healthy as your last meal. Some people get discouraged if they have health problems, are overweight or obese. But if you think about what we have learned about digestion and intermediary metabolism above, it becomes clear that we are as good as our last meal. As our body works through the last meal we ate, we get another chance to bless and restore a healthy balance the next time we eat. Don't forget to call upon or underestimate the importance of the 4th Healer – Food, in adding years to your life and life to your years!

LOCATE YOURSELF

What type of foods do you gravitate towards—living foods, such as fresh fruits and vegetables, or processed foods such as pasta, pastries, cakes, and candy? How many grams of fiber are you getting daily? Is having a bowel movement a regular, daily occurrence or a weekly event? How has this chapter challenged you in the area of your food choices? What changes do you feel you need to make in order to make the most of the food you eat?

A QUICK ENCAPSULATION

Food is Healer #4 and it is the strongest drug you put in your body. While making unhealthy food choices will diminish the quality and quantity of your life, healthy choices will enhance it. Since the body breaks down food into three major forms—carbohydrates, fats, and proteins—it's important to get a percentage of all these nutrients at each meal along with vital micronutrients and adequate fiber. By using the Hand Signals of Health and incorporating the wisdom of this Healer, you can reverse the curse of poor eating one meal at a time.

YOUR SEVEN HEALERS SCORE

Rate yourself on a 1 – 10 scale: 1 – Never, 3 – Sometimes, 5 – Half the time, 7 – Mostly, and 10 – Always, on these two statements;

_____ I use the hand Signals of Health when I eat.

_____ I eat a rainbow of vegetables and fruits at the first part of my meals each day.

_____ I am a success in reducing saturated fat, trans fats, refined carbohydrates, high fructose corn syrup and sugar.

_____ I successfully add monounsaturated fats and deep water fish (or fish oil supplements) to my diet.

_____ I eat balanced meals and snacks (protein, carbohydrate, and fat).

Go to **www.mysevenhealers.com** and get your full Seven Healers Score™ In addition you can find more information on the Fourth Healer and the series Eating to Live and Living to Eat!

Recommended Resources: *Eating Well for Optimum Health* by Andrew Weil, M.D. (New York, Alfred A. Knopf: 2000). *Fast Food Nation* by Eric Schlosser (New York, NY: Harper Perennial, 2004).

(1) Andrew Weil, M.D., Eating Well for Optimum Health (New York, NY, Alfred A. Knopf: 2000) p.9.

(2) Definition of Drug (http://medical-dictionary.thefreedictionary.com/drug, retrieved 2-18-10). (3) See The Bible, John 6:32-35, 51.

"...Our bodies are approximately two-thirds water. ...When water moves, life thrives. Running water is usually fresh water. Rivers and waterfalls are beautiful and inviting—alive. That's a perfect picture of what exercise does. It refreshes your body and clears it of toxins and cellular garbage, sharpening your mind and giving you strength and energy. ...Exercise is the remedy to prevent death and stir the waters of life in our bodies."

Don Colbert, M.D.[1]

RAPHAFIVE PLAY

You will become sick, miserable, and depressed
without *play.*

Your body was made to move, and *play* is all about movement. Just about
any form of activity or exercise can be categorized as play. Why are we
calling it *play* instead of exercise? Because when most people think of
exercise, they think of tedious and tiring work, and who wants to do that?
Instead, let's have some fun! Let's move our body and play—that's what
really counts!

An interesting study was conducted by Dr. Blair at the Cooper
Aerobics Institute in Dallas, Texas. He looked at answering the question:
Is it better to have a lower weight but be out of shape or be heavier and in
shape with regard to heart health and how long we live? The answer was
people who had a lower weight and were out of shape did not do as well
as those who were heavier but in shape! Of course, those that were at a
healthy weight *and* fit did the best, and those that were heavy and not fit did
the worst. So focusing on getting fit, even if your weight is still somewhat
elevated, is a great place to start. As Dr Kenneth Cooper himself states, "The
reason I exercise is for the quality of life I enjoy."

Too many people get hung up on what a workout should be instead of just getting out there and doing something. If you were to lie in bed and do nothing, your body would eventually develop fatal blood clots and painful osteoporosis (thinning of the bones). The less you move, the less you want to move and the less you are able to move. Therefore, finding your way to continue to *play* is imperative. If the activity you are doing is fun, you will keep doing it, and it will perpetuate itself. And the good news is, play doesn't have to be strenuous to be beneficial. Every activity counts and adds value to your life!

activity reduces toxicity

Now, you may be thinking, *is going to the park and playing with my kids or grandkids on the slide and swings and rolling in the grass really beneficial?* Yes, in a number of ways. For starters, it causes you to breathe deeply, which in turn oxygenates your body and gives your heart and lungs a workout. It also supports your lymphatic system—the all-important drainage system that purges your body of impurities. As we learned earlier, when you take a deep breath, it creates a vacuum in your chest that draws lymphatic fluid out of your tissues toward your chest. This yellowish-colored, toxin-filled fluid then empties into the venous system and is eventually eliminated as waste by the kidneys and liver.

In addition to deep breathing, the movement of our muscles also supports the flow of blood and lymphatic fluid through our body. When we play, we use our muscles, and the fibers shorten and squeeze together. This pushes the fluid and toxins out of our muscles and into the veins and lymphatic channels. For instance, when you flex your leg muscles, they squeeze the blood and lymphatic vessels within the muscle. This pushes the blood and lymphatic fluid out of the muscle and up your leg and toward your chest. To prevent flow back down the leg the veins and channels have one-way valves. Once the fluid makes it through a valve, it cannot flow backwards down toward your feet. When your muscles relax, a vacuum is created inside the muscle that draws fresh blood and fluid into the muscle to make sure there is plenty of fuel in the form of oxygen and sugar available. This process sets your muscles, as well as your entire body, up for success.

When people stay in one position that requires their muscles to remain flexed for a long period of time, such as sitting bent over at a desk, toxins build up in the tissues and fresh oxygen and energy flow are reduced. Over time, this will cause these muscles to spasm. That's why many people who do a lot of sitting develop trigger points of pain in their neck, shoulders, and back. They are not using their muscles the way they were intended to be used.

One great solution is a simple massage. It will force toxins out of the muscles, increasing good blood flow and relieving pain.

To those who sit at a desk for hours on end, I encourage you to get up periodically and flex your muscles and stretch. The fact is, our minds struggle to maintain an intense focus after about forty-five minutes. At that point, we need a break. Whether you have five, ten, or fifteen minutes, use your muscles. Take a brief walk, stretch, or squeeze the muscle of your upper back and neck. The more muscles you use throughout the day the better. Moving and flexing your back, chest, legs, arms, buttocks, abdomen, etc, will really help push toxins out of your tissues and draw fresh energy into them.

play produces many positive results

Without a doubt, *exercise or play is the best medicine for the body*. Studies have been done on people suffering from both depression and anxiety in which some of the participants were given medication and others were told to exercise. Researchers discovered that both medication and exercise worked *equally* well at reducing the symptoms of anxiety and depression. However, when the medication and exercise were stopped after six months, they found that those who did the exercises did not get depressed as quickly again. On the other hand, those on medication tended to move right back into depression.

Not only is exercise a great antidepressant, it is also a major stress releaser. Whether we are a stay-at-home mom, a factory worker, or a business executive, most of us are intensely focused at our jobs all day long. It's true that we have to be professional and get our job done, but without play, our lives become too serious. When we play and are active, we re-establish the balance of our stress hormones, such as epinephrine and norepinephrine. This enables our whole body to relax. When we have play in our routine, we give our body an outlet to release stress.

Exercise and regular activity also set us up for ongoing success. During play, our body burns fuel in the form of sugar and fat. Once we are done what was used is "restocked" and the body replenishes it. This action goes on for many hours *after* you exercise. Then at night, when you enter deep sleep, stage N3, your growth hormone (HGH) level peaks, and your body burns even more energy to repair the muscle that was broken down during the day. That's one of the greatest long-term benefits of exercise—you burn calories at the time of exercise, prime your system to pull fat and sugar out of your bloodstream for replenishment immediately after, and increase the total number of calories you burn for the next twenty-four to forty eight hours. This is all because you regularly chose to go play a little!

Another benefit of play is that it strengthens our heart and blood vessels (circulatory system). When you are active, your heart pumps more, and as a result your blood vessels stay younger and stronger. The more you activate and stimulate your heart and blood vessels, the longer you live as your heart and blood vessels stay in shape instead of becoming corroded with plaque and dysfunctional.

Think about it. When you are exercising your body, what are you doing? You are taking deep breaths, moving your muscles, and more than likely drinking a lot more water. You are also sweating and moving toxins out of your body through respiration, urination, digestion, and perspiration - so three Healers— *air*, *water*, and *play*—are synergistically working together to keep your body fit and free from toxicity. When play is done with friends, you bring the 6th Healer, relationships, on board. And if being fit and healthy contributes to achieving your life goals, you also bring in the 7th Healer—purpose.

Play in the Form of Regular Exercise Provides You with…

- Increased energy
- Better sleep
- A stronger immune system
- Reduced stress, anxiety and depression
- Stabilized blood pressure and blood sugar levels
- Improved digestion
- Regular bowel movements
- Healthy heart, bones, and blood vessels
- Better memory retention and a sharper mind

---

weight training results in rapid rewards

One of the best forms of activity you can do is weight training. I used to think that all the "muscle heads" who lifted weights weren't really accomplishing very much, but that is not true. The benefits of weightlifting are far-reaching and include better posture, stronger joints and joint support, and the increased release of the "feel-good" hormones dopamine and serotonin. Through regular weight training, our bone density increases, which fights off osteoporosis. Likewise, our muscle density increases, strengthening our body and improving our ability to burn excess fat. Over a twenty-four hour period, our muscles actually burn *ten times* more calories than fat. The number of calories we burn in a twenty-four-hour period is directly proportional to our muscle mass. When we turn 1 pound of fat into 1 pound of muscle, we increase our basal metabolic rate (BMR)—the rate at which our body changes food into usable energy.

Another incredible thing that occurs during our workout and times of activity is our blood gets healthier. As we repeatedly flex and relax our muscles, we stimulate and activate our P-PAR Gamma receptors. These net-like receptors located within each of our cells extend themselves into the bloodstream, capturing and consuming fresh energy in the form of fat and sugar. This activity effectively helps to lower our blood sugar and cholesterol levels and lasts one to two days *after* exercising, depending on how hard and long we play. So we definitely want to use as many muscles as we can every one or two days to keep this invigorating process going.

Indeed, weight training gives you great, rapid feedback, which makes a big difference in how you look and feel. You don't have to go to the gym and push yourself. Just doing twenty minutes of weightlifting three times a week will bring noticeable improvements in your overall quality of life. Personally, I enjoy meeting my friends early in the morning at the gym. Not only do we work out with weights, we also talk and share our experiences. Again, exercising with friends and family can be very powerful because it also incorporates the sixth Healer, *relationships*, which we will talk about in the next chapter.

As you begin weight training, I recommend that you get a trainer. They will help you learn the mechanics of how your body works, as well as how to do the right exercises on the right machines with the right amount of weight to produce the right results. In this way, you will be placed on a program that is both safe and fun, and at the same time you will be accountable to someone else.

"Even modest physical activity can make your Real Age younger—substantially younger. A study published in the Journal of the American Medical Association found that one of the key reasons Americans don't exercise is the common misconception that a person needs to do taxing and rigorous workouts to reap benefits. That's simply not true. Almost all of us would benefit greatly by just boosting our overall physical activity."
—*Michael F. Roizen, M.D.*[3]

every step counts

For many Americans, life is very sedentary, or inactive. In fact on average, patients in my practice only take about 3,000 to 3,500 steps per day. This is low when compared to the national goal of 10,000 steps per day. The importance of this can be appreciated when patients wear pedometers and go from 3,000 to 10,000 steps a day. Their weight drops, cholesterol and blood pressure get better, and they feel more alert and alive. The effects of a change in the number of steps can also be seen when this trend goes the other way.

I worked with a couple from India who had relocated to the United States. In India, they were both very active, walking all day long. However, they quickly gained 30 pounds after they came to America. What was even worse was that the man's cholesterol level rose significantly, and his wife became a full-blown diabetic. Interestingly, their diet hadn't changed very much. The cause for their weight gain was simply the drastic decrease in their level of activity. Clearly, when we have little to no activity in our life, there are significant consequences. While some people experience high cholesterol or high blood pressure, others develop diabetes. And most of the time, people gain weight.

The good news is, *any* motion or activity counts! Walking, stretching, and playing with your children or grandchildren all add value to your life. Repetitive motions burn calories and keep muscles burning fat and sugar. Just moving your fingers up and down will burn 11 calories a day. Likewise, research has shown that people who cross their legs while seated and shake one of them up and down, weigh about 3 pounds less than someone who does not continually move their leg.

What can you do to take some steps in the right direction? I encourage you to begin walking more and using a pedometer to count your steps. As you increase your steps from 3,000 to 6,000 per day, you will arrive at a "break even" point, meaning you won't gain additional weight. By raising your daily step count to 10,000, you will be in a position of actually losing weight. The more regular activity you are involved in, the better your health will be.

take it slow and steady

Remember, play doesn't have to be strenuous to be effective. If you are out of shape or overweight and want to become physically fit, *slowly* begin to incorporate new activities in your life. Play with your kids or grandkids more, get outdoors, and move your body regularly every other day. Begin developing a routine of deep breathing, stretching, and walking. If you try to do too much too quickly, you will become extremely sore and probably won't want to continue.

I remember when I first began doing regular activity and discovered the power of play. My wife and I went on a walk, and I couldn't keep up with her. She left me in the dust, which was quite humiliating. I couldn't believe how far I had let my health deteriorate. In an effort to regain control, I began walking regularly. I then started some light weightlifting. Through it all, my wife was very supportive and so were my friends.

Ironically, one of the guys I was walking with challenged me to run a marathon. Initially I thought, *What a joke! I am a middle-aged, out-of-shape man who can barely keep up with my wife. There's no way I can run a marathon.* Nevertheless, over the next several months, I slowly moved from walking to jogging and increased my distance in small increments. I also began to turn myself over to someone greater than me for help by repeating the Prayer of Jabez repetitively while exercising. Amazingly, my endurance and energy levels increased, and many of my lifestyle choices changed. Not only did I run in that marathon, I also ran in three others!

how often should we play?

The answer is, every twenty-four to forty-eight hours, which translates to at least every other day. If you play hard twenty to thirty minutes at least three times per week, you will live longer than if you don't play at all. Again, as you start, start slowly and don't overdo it. Pace yourself and have fun. Enjoy the process of creating a new lifestyle. Once you feel an increase in your energy level and your body becomes stronger, gradually intensify your play and add some new activities to your play menu. Consistency is the key, and variety will keep your activities fresh and fun. Drink plenty of water, and exercise with a friend when possible.

"Brisk walking is one of the best exercises I can recommend, and it's virtually free. It can give you three times the normal amount of oxygen you would otherwise get. . . . Walking is a form of aerobic exercise. Aerobic means 'in the presence of air.' It's the kind of exercise that gets you breathing deeply and more rapidly than normal. Aerobic exercises generally work the large muscle groups of the body in repetitive motions for a sustained period of time."
—Don Colbert, M.D.[2]

Don't exercise right after you eat or right before you go to bed. Exercising immediately after a meal will interfere with your digestion, and exercising right before going to bed may cause you to be unable to sleep.

Some other helpful tips to incorporate movement into your day include parking further away from the door at work and the supermarket. You can also opt to take the stairs instead of the elevator. Remember, some movement is better than no movement, and all activities add value to your life. So get up, get out, and get moving. Don't be stagnant. Whatever form of play you choose—walking, swimming, jogging, dancing, weightlifting, hiking, or biking—do something that's fun and makes your muscles move. Your body will thank you for it!

LOCATE YOURSELF
What type of activities are you presently doing? Do you enjoy them? If not, what other form of play do you think you would enjoy? If you have exercised or played sports on a regular basis, what benefits do you remember receiving from it? What can you do to incorporate play in your routine more?

A QUICK ENCAPSULATION
Play is Healer #5, and it is basically any activity or exercise. It is the best medicine for your body, and it doesn't have to be strenuous to be beneficial. Every activity counts and adds value to your life. Regular activity reduces toxicity by activating the lymphatic system. It also reduces the symptoms of anxiety and depression, devours excess stress hormones, strengthens your circulatory system, and activates your P-PAR Gamma receptors that effectively help lower your blood sugar and cholesterol levels. As you aim to play every other day for twenty to thirty minutes, you will reap the rich rewards that follow!

YOUR SEVEN HEALERS SCORE
Rate yourself on a 1 – 10 scale: 1 – Never, 3 – Sometimes, 5 – Half the time, 7 – Mostly, and 10 – Always, on these statements;

____ I am active and play for at least 150 minutes per week or over 6000 steps/day.

____ I incorporate resistance training (e.g. weight lifting, sit ups pushups), aerobic activity (e.g. running, biking, or swimming) and flexibility (e.g. stretching, yoga, or Pilate's) exercises into my exercise program.

Recommended Resources: *Real Age, Are You As Young As You Can Be?* by Michael F. Roizen, M.D. (New York, NY: HarperCollins Publishers, Inc.: 1999). *Enter the Zone* by Barry Sears (New York, NY: HarperCollins, 1995).

(1) Don Colbert, M.D., The Seven Pillars of Health (Lake Mary, FL: Siloam, 2007) pp.117-118. (2) See note 1, p. 127. (3) Michael F. Roizen, M.D., Real Age, Are You As Young As You Can Be? (New York, NY: HarperCollins Publishers, Inc.: 1999) p. 212.

"I used to do a considerable amount of counseling, and if there's one thing I learned from those interactions, it's that our *relationships* very often define who we are and what we can become."

John C. Maxwell[1]

RAPHASIX RELATIONSHIPS

You will die much sooner without loving *relationships.*

Life is about relationships, and *Relationships* is Healer #6. When I first started teaching my patients who were trying to lose weight about the Seven Healers, I had a few participants who were "Ph.D.s" in the first five. They knew and were incorporating the wisdom of air, water, sleep, food, and play. However, they never reached their weight loss goals because the last two healers—Relationships and Purpose – were working against them. They either had toxic relationships that held them back, or they didn't have a clear sense of how losing weight would contribute to them fulfilling the purpose of their lives

Indeed, without healthy, loving relationships, we will not have a meaningful life. Many people work themselves silly trying to accumulate great fortune or fame, but when the end of their life comes, most of what they worked so long and hard for feels incomplete or meaningless. I have never had a person who was lying on their deathbed say to me, "I'm sure glad I worked those extra 2 hours every day," or "Man, am I so glad I bought the home with 500 square feet more in it." Although these things may have felt important at the time, they never come up in conversation when someone is dying. On the contrary, the number one thing people talk about is their relationships.

While just about every hurt we experience comes through people, so does the most beneficial and blessed experiences. Love, acceptance, companionship, encouragement, comfort, compassion, wisdom, and other valuable resources, all come into our lives through relationships. Let's take a closer look at how relationships affect and direct our lives, what relationships are most important, and how you can make the most out of this powerful healer.

identifying the person closest to you

Who is the person you spend the most time with? Do the most with? Have the hardest time accepting? The closest and strongest relationship you have is the one *with yourself*. It's kind of like we each have an internal trinity—*me*, *myself*, and *I*. No matter where you go, whether you are awake or asleep, in a crowd or alone at home, "you" are always with you. Therefore, as odd as it sounds, it is imperative that you learn how to accept and get along with yourself. The healthier your relationship is with you, the healthier your relationship will be with others. If you don't like yourself, you are going to have problems.

Unfortunately, there are many people who simply don't like themselves. It could be the result of growing up in a dysfunctional family, having continual conflict with peers, or experiencing verbal, physical, or sexual abuse. Whatever the case may be, we have to come to peace with the situations and grow beyond them. The truth is as our minds develop from birth to adulthood we have periods when we are vulnerable and we learn hard lessons by making mistakes, or having by others make mistakes in our relationships – and it hurts. Everybody on the planet has experienced what they consider mistreatment and abuse at the hands of those they care most about in their lives. Yet, in spite of what we have been through, we can learn how to push past the pain and choose to respond in a healthy way. Viktor Frankl, survivor of a torturous Nazi concentration camp during WWII, said it best, declaring,

> "Everything can be taken from a man or a woman but one thing: the last of human freedoms to choose one's attitude in any given set of circumstances, to choose one's own way."[2]

Instead of using the abuse and mistreatment he endured as a reason to give up on life or be critical and angry at the world, Viktor saw it as the key element to motivate him toward staying alive and becoming free; and the same opportunity is available to you. You can draw a line between you and the pain of the past and begin to receive internal healing. As you break free, you will discover hope for the future and freedom from the mistakes of the past.

so how do you feel about *you*?

One of the ways we can gauge the health of our relationship with ourselves is by examining the way we talk to ourselves. In other words, what is the tone and content of our thoughts—the internal conversation going on in our mind? You know…the "itty-bitty committee" that never seems to adjourn in our heads. The thoughts we think about ourselves, about others, and about every situation and challenge we face. Our opinions and actions, when they are based upon our thoughts, are the product of doing the best we can to figure out and understand the importance of the thoughts and experiences we have collected over the duration of our lifetime.

That being said, here's a powerful point I don't want you to miss. The information and thoughts we have about our past and what happened is often inaccurate and untrue. Given the fact that the world's understanding and knowledge doubles every 36 months today it is not surprising that, in some cases, our present perspective is based on out-dated information that is inaccurate. In addition, the thoughts and perspectives we had about the things that happened in our lives when we were much younger, say five years old, were completely appropriate for a five year old, but now that we are thirty, forty, or fifty-something if we were to have had the same experience it would have a completely different affect on us, and we would have a whole different set of memories and experiences. So to the degree we base our lives—opinions and actions—on our thoughts, we are likely to be misguided and incomplete in our understanding and insights.

If you think about it, for most of us, our relationship with ourselves and others is occurring all the time in our stream of thought. We then act it out externally in the way that we treat ourselves and others. Becoming aware of this process is extremely valuable to our overall quality of life. By monitoring our stream of thought, we can choose *not* to act on thoughts that may be antiquated and/or incorrect. Consequently, as we pay attention to our thoughts about ourselves and others, and open ourselves to other perspectives and new knowledge, a new way of relating to ourselves and others will emerge and we will find significant improvement in our relationships.

so how's your relationship with you?

Are you often irritated, aggravated, and frustrated with yourself? Do you frequently feel guilty, ashamed, or condemned about the things you say and do? Are you holding onto bitterness, anger, or hatred toward yourself? One of the best ways to measure the health of your relationship with you is to look at how you treat your body, especially regarding the first five healers. Think for a moment and ask yourself…

- "How's my breathing? Is it fast-paced and shallow? Do I smoke or use drugs?"

- "How about water? Do I take in what my body needs, or do I drink a lot of unhealthy liquids?"

- "Am I getting enough sleep, or am I barely getting by with the least amount of shut-eye?"

- "What kind of foods am I eating on a regular basis? Are they living foods that are full of vitamins, minerals and phytonutrients? Or are they dead foods that are processed, refined, and full of fat and sugar?"

- "What about play? Do I have regular activity and exercise in my life, or am I a couch potato?"

- And last, but certainly not least, "*Do I care if my body is harmed*—do I really care about my overall health or do I just want what I want when I want it?"

The answers to these questions will help reveal how you really feel about you.

To improve your relationships with others, you must first improve your relationship with yourself. As the timeless truth states, you are to "…love your neighbor *as* you do yourself."[3] If you don't love yourself in a balanced, healthy way, you really are powerless to love anyone else. You can't share or give away what you don't have. So the key to having good relationships with others begins by having a good relationship with yourself.

If you walk into a room with dozens of people speaking different languages where will you tend to move to? In all likelihood you will find the people who speak English, those you can relate to and understand.

The people in the room speaking other languages will be ignored or avoided. In our lives we do the same thing. In our conversation in our minds we have a language and way of speaking to ourselves. There are things we recognize and are comfortable spending time around, and those we are not. In our lives we will seek out and find people who "speak our language" while avoiding those who do not. Ever wonder why the same, or similar things keep happening to you over and over again? It is not an accident, we seek out and thus make sure things are set up a certain way. An abusive boyfriend or girlfriend, too much alcohol or drugs, a dead end job, not exercising or taking care of ourselves. Success in the future will come when we move into deeper appreciation of who we are, how we got here, and an openness to relationships that may feel "Greek" when you first begin them, but soon result in seeing ourselves and our worlds in new, and inviting ways.

your relationship with others

Okay, so how about our relationships with others? What effect does it have upon the quality of our lives? The answer is quite a bit. As the ageless book of Proverbs proclaims, "Become wise by walking with the wise; hang out with fools and watch your life fall to pieces."[4] Indeed, who we hang out with has a definite effect on the direction and the destiny of our lives. Show me your friends and I'll show you your future.

I remember a woman who came to one of our weight loss classes who started losing a lot of weight. Shortly thereafter, some of her friends, who were not in the class, began taking her out to lunch at all-you-can eat buffets. Why did they do this? It was probably for a number of reasons. They may have felt insecure, inferior, jealous, or envious. Whatever the case, they didn't want their friend to be successful at losing weight. Although they never specifically said to her, "Hey, we don't want you to lose weight," they very subtly communicated their disapproval by making sure she always had candy, food, and a complimentary ride to her favorite restaurants—the places they knew she would overeat. Consequently, they undermined her success.

This is a clear example of a dysfunctional relationship. Other common indicators of an unhealthy relationship include stress, guilt, emotional eating, anger, and frequent frustration with a certain person. Sometimes we don't even realize the effect negative relationships are having in our lives. Oftentimes, when people continue to hold onto or "stuff" their negative emotions, they build up inside, and when they finally do come out, they take the form of pain and disease somewhere in their body. Depression, anxiety, headaches, stomach aches, ulcers, insomnia, chest pain, and muscle tension when you are around a certain person are all symptoms revealing that you are not handling a relationship well. When you no longer enjoy being around someone you were once good friends with, something has shifted, something has changed. It may be that you are becoming aware of their affect on you and are looking for a better, more positive, less stressed out life.

There are some people we get in relationship with who suck the life right out of us. Let's call them "emotional vampires." They often make statements like, "I'm doing this for your own good," "You're so important; I don't know what I'd do without you," "If you really love me, you would…," and the classic, "You owe me because I…." When you hear energy-draining statements like these, beware. It's time to say no to their request and establish a boundary in your relationship. This will break their control over your life. If they are unwilling to abide by the boundary you set, distance yourself from them. If this person is your spouse or child, it will be more of a challenge, but there are ways to deal with it and not cut them off, and over the long haul you are actually helping both them and yourself by enforcing clear boundaries.

By looking at your friends and seeing how they live their lives, you can get a good idea of what your life is going to be like in the near future (if it isn't that way already). How healthy are they? Do they get sick often? What kind of foods do they eat? What kind of habits do they have? Are they work-a-holics? Do they exercise? What are their standards, values, and beliefs? How is their relationship with their husband or wife and with their children? The bottom line: Are your friends living the life you imagined and want? If not, I strongly encourage you to begin looking for new relationships to balance off or replace the effect of these "friends." As the Good Book says,

"Do not be misled: 'Bad company corrupts good character."
1 Corinthians 15:33 NIV

The key to having good relationships is to recruit friends that are earnestly striving to live the quality of life you want. Healthy relationships motivate you to be the best you can be in all areas of life. A good friend will not condone your wrong choices, but they will also not condemn you for them. They will hold you accountable for your actions, bring encouragement when you need it, provide support and guidance for important decisions, ask hard questions when they feel you are off track, and celebrate your successes in life. I truly believe this is what the ancient proverb means: "As iron sharpens iron, so a man sharpens the countenance of his friend."

the ultimate relationship

After living nearly half a century and practicing medicine for over twenty-two years , I have come to the realization that *every* person has a spiritual side to their life that cannot be ignored—a "God-hole" that must be filled in order to achieve optimum health. Now, I realize that acknowledging God flies in the face of some people—it did for me too many years ago. But I ask you to hear me out.

My father was a family doctor and practiced medicine for many years in Florida. He was trained in the scientific method which worked well in his practice, limiting his reliance on God for success. Working from this mind set he seemed to be more agnostic in his beliefs and actions for much of his earlier life. But one day when I was young, he told me something I will never forget. He said, "Scott, I can't 100 percent prove to you in a textbook that God exists, but what I *can* tell you is that the people I know who practice a relationship with God live a different and often a better, more content and satisfied life than those who don't."

Again and again, he witnessed the same scenario play out before him: When a deathly-ill person he was caring for had faith in God, they did not experience the panic or anxiety-related disorders and complications that most people without faith in God went through. The way these faith-filled people lived their life and how they dealt with adversity impacted him greatly. More and more, he came to realize that there was something at work in these people that was much more powerful that just a simple belief or blind faith.

A turning point for my father took place one night when he was working late at the hospital. At that time, he had a patient who was battling for his life in the intensive care unit (ICU). At some point, the man coded, which means his heart stopped. Immediately, Dad rushed into action with the other doctors and nurses on duty, working quickly they were able to resuscitate this patient using CPR. Almost instantly, the man opened his eyes and looked at my dad and said, "What in the world do you think you are doing? I was in a place of complete peace on my way to reunite with my wife. Please, don't stop me!" Five minutes later his heart stopped again and the man died In that moment, a powerful, supernatural presence filled the room. Needless to say, my dad was deeply impacted by this experience. After witnessing events like this, he turned his life over to God and has been in relationship with Him ever since.

87

A *Relationship* with a Good Friend Is a source of…

- **SUPPORT** in times of difficulty
- **ACCOUNTABILITY** to overcome bad habits and stay committed
- **SAFETY & SECURITY** in troubling, uncertain situations
- **ENCOURAGEMENT & MOTIVATION** when discouragement comes
- **WISDOM & DIRECTION** in making life's decisions
- **LAUGHTER & FUN** to celebrate your accomplishments
- **PERSPECTIVE** to see things you can't see on your own

As you receive these things from others, look for opportunities to give to others too.

a whole new world

Of course, you are totally free to chose, or ignore a spiritual part of your life. There was time in my life when I had no regard for God at all. In fact, I believed science itself was god. But through a series of events and situations, my heart was changed. For me it began with the realization that science is based upon matter and energy already existing – but there is no explanation for where the first mass and energy emerged. What or who was the "unmoved mover" that created the universe and set it in motion? My first step was to admit that the god I was living my life by had a significant hole, so it was logical to me that whatever the force was that made the first matter/energy was beyond anything we currently could explain. Thus there had to be an unmoved mover, a God.

Through the experiences I will describe in the Conclusion my perspective shifted from reliance on myself and the god called science, to the reality that, for my life to change (something I had a strong desire to achieve) a shift had to occur. I was very angry and frustrated with my life, and the decisions that I had made. I was stuck in a bad relationship with myself, and this lead to bad relationships with others. So first I had to forgive myself for the mistakes I had made. To the degree I was trapped, listening to my "itty-bitty commitee" to figure out what I needed to do, I was very incomplete, and often using outdated and inaccurate information to base my life on. But the force that created everything and understands all there is to understand, from His comprehensive understanding it all makes perfect sense. My understanding is very limited, His is not. I am way too incomplete in my understanding to judge others; I know too little and am too fraught with my personal biases and incompleteness. Other people, in the context of their internal conversations, are doing what they know to do, based on their limited and incomplete information too. I see the innocence and limitations of their way of being, just as I see it for myself, and thus I continually try not to cast judgment. From this perspective it is easy to forgive them, and myself. It is in this place of humility and appreciation that I have come to experience a dynamic and free life. I am more aware and sensitive to the effect I have on others and their effect on me, and so I try to live in a way to have a more beneficial effect on their lives and I am paid back with riches and in ways I could never imagine.

In the Christian tradition that I follow, it is believed that the relationship with God is dynamic and goes two ways. God loves you too and wants to build a relationship with you that is beyond your wildest dreams. He says, "Look! I have been standing at the door and I am constantly knocking. If anyone hears me calling him and opens the door, I will come in and fellowship with him and he with me."[6] If I will open my heart to Him, quit relying on my limited understanding to live my life, and turn myself over to His keeping, my life takes on a whole new meaning.

Does this mean life will be free from all trouble and heart ache? No, but when something difficult does occur, there is comfort, understanding and peace that sticks closer than a brother by my side to support me through. "And we know that God causes everything to work together for the good of those who love God and are called according to his purpose for them."[7]

Another key aspect of the Christian tradition is that a good relationship with God is not about acts or service – these come, not from a great relationship, but rather in believing in and receiving His forgiveness. He demonstrated His commitment to forgive us by sending His Son, Jesus Christ literally to choose to die a painful and public death to show us his commitment to us, and to have it recorded for all to know and appreciate; stating again and again that he is doing this so we will know that we are forgiven. Jesus himself said it to us repetitively while walking the earth: I love you, I am taking away your sins (literally the places where you have missed the target). Repent (literally, aim again), know you are forgiven, for the kingdom of God is at hand (here and now for you to experience through love and forgiveness). I do this for you in the honor of my God.

This leads to tremendous freedom. When we stop "playing God" ourselves, see our limitations, not as a curse or bad thing, but rather as a condition of being a human being, a burden is lifted from our shoulders. When we start to walk in self forgiveness, appreciating who we are, challenging ourselves to repent (aim again) where we fall, knowing that the force that created the universe is on our side and will be with us on our walk. All there is to do is to seek, knock, and ask for His guidance.

In this tradition, once you receive this forgiveness, you will forgive yourself. This is your starting point for healthy relationships. Instead of having a mindset that thinks, *I'm damaged goods; I'm an incomplete person. I mess up all the time and it causes harm to others without my even knowing at times, or on the other hand, thinking "I am perfect, I know what to do in my life." Both mindsets often result in hurt relationships with others and loneliness ourselves.* Imagine a life that starts with, "I am who I am, and I'm forgiven. God loves and accepts me, and if He loves and accepts me, I can love and accept myself and others too." Indeed, standing in this place and living life improves every relationship and empowers us to identify and fulfill our Purpose (the 7th Healer) in life!

LOCATE YOURSELF

How would you describe your relationship with yourself? If it's not healthy, what do you think you can do to improve it? What relationships in your life would you describe as toxic that you need to distance yourself from? Who are you in relationship with that motivates you to live healthy and be the best you can be? Do you have a relationship with God? If you do, how would you describe it? If you don't, why?

A QUICK ENCAPSULATION

Relationships is Healer #6. Without healthy, loving relationships, we will not have a meaningful life. Clearly, the company we keep powerfully impacts our direction and destiny. If your friends are not living the life you imagined or want, you need to look for new ones. Keep in mind that in order to improve your relationships, you have to first improve your relationship with yourself. And having a good relationship with yourself begins with having a restored relationship with God. Knowing you are forgiven, accepted, and loved sets you free to be all you can be and build relationships that are life-giving!

Recommended Resources: (*Boundaries* by Dr. Henry Cloud and Dr. John Townsend (Grand Rapids, MI, Zondervan Publishing House: 1992). *The Bait of Satan* by John Bevere (Lake Mary, FL: Charisma House, 1997).)

YOUR SEVEN HEALERS SCORE

Rate yourself on a 1 – 10 scale: 1 – Never, 3 – Sometimes, 5 – Half the time, 7 – Mostly, and 10 – Always, on these statements;

_____ I spend time with friends who call me to be my best and encourage me in my life.

_____ I give without expectation to the people I come in contact with.

_____ I forgive myself and others for things that don't go well.

Go to **www.mysevenhealers.com** and get your full Seven Healers Score™

A fable:

A man had a beautiful stallion in a rural community many year ago. The towns people came to him and said "you should sell the horse and become wealthy for if you do not you will be poor all of your life." He said "I do not want to sell my horse." One day the horse ran away and the towns people said "see we told you so," and he said "all we know is that my horse is no longer here." Several weeks later the stallion returned with 10 mares and the towns people said "you were right, you are now even more wealthy," to which he replied "all we know is that I now have more horses—why do you seek to assign significance to what happens in life?" Soon thereafter his son broke his hip trying to break one of the mares and the towns people said "you were right the mares were not a blessing," to which he replied "this may be, we do not know." A month later war was declared in his country and all able bodied young men had to go serve, many of them dying and the towns people declared "you were blessed and your son did not have to serve, you are lucky," to which he dropped his head in amazement and said "you see with such limited eyes, why do you not understand that it is not for us to know? Why do you chose to live such judgmental lives?"

(1) "Relational Refueling," Dr. John C. Maxwell, Enjoying Everyday Life magazine, June 2005 (Joyce Meyer Ministries, Inc., Fenton, MO) p. 19. (2) Quotes by Vicktor Frankl (http://www.brainyquote.com/quotes/authors/v/viktor_e_frankl.html, retrieved 3-16-10). (3) See the Bible, Matthew 19:19 The Message. (4) See the Bible, Proverbs 13:20 The Message. (5) See the Bible, Proverbs 27:17 NKJV. (6) See the Bible, Revelation 3:20 TLB. (7) See the Bible, Romans 8:28 NLT. (8) See the Bible, Romans 10:19; 1 John 1:9; 4:15. (9) See the Bible, Exodus 20:1-17; Romans 3:23.

"I'm not convinced that your date of death is the date carved on your tombstone. Most people die long before that. We start dying when we have nothing worth living for. And we don't really start living until we find something worth dying for. Ironically, discovering something worth dying for is what makes life worth living."

Mark Batterson[1]

RAPHA**SEVEN** PURPOSE

Living life without *purpose* is an empty,
short-lived existence.

The last healer we want to focus on is *purpose*, the vital, life-building and sustaining healer that provides the "why" behind everything we do. It is the thing that gets us up in the morning when nothing else will. The less purpose a person has discovered, the less they care about their life, and the more they wander aimlessly through life. When you get down to it, a person without purpose really doesn't care about breathing right, eating right, or getting enough water or sleep. They just trudge along without a context to gauge the meaning or significance of their actions.

Interestingly, the word *purpose* is defined as "that which a person sets before himself as an object to be reached or accomplished." In other words, purpose is like the bull's-eye on a target that an archer or marksman takes aim at. Without purpose, we are shooting randomly. The word purpose also carries with it the idea of *intention* and *design*. Nature (God) designed us with a very specific and personal set of tools and skills. Why? What is the intention of our life? Of all the billions of possibilities, why did we turn out just as we did?

To discover our destiny, we must go back to where we left off in the last chapter, and that is having great relationships, which begins with letting go of the attitude that we know enough to judge others and ourselves. We switch from being a "knower" to a "learner." This is a significant shift. It moves us from living our lives recreating (or looking for) what we are familiar with or used to (our past), where things happened to us and we survived, so we know what happens if we repeat that script (with different circumstances and people, but basically a new chapter of the same old book). This way of living life feels "safe;" ultimately, we always know what is going to happen—we are actually subconsciously directing the script. Once we give this up, we become open to the possibility of living life a different way. This means we give up knowing what will happen, thus being open to new scripts being written, not by ourselves, but by what our lives "pull for." In other words, we become open to having exciting, vibrant, unexpected, and often miraculous things occur in our life that we never imagined were possible.

tap into your purpose

Let's look at this one more time: How much do we really know? Take a pen and a piece of paper and draw a large circle on it that fills the page. Pretend the circle represents all the knowledge there is to know in the universe (if you are spiritual – literally all that the creator – God – knows). Out of all this information, how much would you say you know?

For the sake of this example, let's be generous and say about 1 percent. From the center of the circle, draw a very small sliver, or pie piece, representing your 1 percent. This symbolizes all the information and your opinions about the information that you have gathered in your mind up to this point.

Of all the remaining knowledge, there are some things that *you know* you *don't know*, such as how to speak Swahili or the top five profit-yielding commodities on the stock market last year. However, you could go find and learn this information. Yes, it would take time, but it is doable. My point is that there is another segment of insight that *you know* you *don't know*. For the sake of our example, let's estimate it to be about 4 percent. To represent this in our circle, carve out a slightly larger sliver next to your 1 percent.

So what are you left with? A massive amount of information that you *don't know* that *you don't know*—say 95 percent. How do you access this enormous wedge of wisdom? Again, it is in coming to the end of yourself and living your life a new and different way—one based on starting from "I don't know" as opposed to starting from "I know" how to live my life. By doing this, you relinquish your status of being a "knower," thinking you have all the answers, and adopt the position of being a "learner" where you learn to lean into new ideas and new ways to do things in your life.

So, if you are spiritual, in a very real sense, when you get out of your 1 percent and into the 99 percent, you are "turning to God"—turning to all there is to know that no one person or group of people alive knows. And if (or when) you find answers, or truths, in this space, we could then say that you are "hearing the voice of God." King Solomon, one of the wisest and wealthiest men to ever live, penned a powerful statement that this is the right way to live. He proclaimed,

> *"Trust God from the bottom of your heart*; don't try to figure out everything on your own. Listen for God's voice in everything you do, everywhere you go; he's the one who will keep you on track. Don't assume that you know it all. Run to God! Run from evil! Your body will glow with HEALTH, your very bones will vibrate with life!"
> Proverbs 3:5-8 The Message

So how do we "run to God" and "run from evil"? Following the truth found in these four verses will transform the way we live. Does turning your life over to God mean you will never fall back into old unhealthy habits? No. It just means that you have made a solid decision to deposit yourself into "His keeping" (the 99 percent) and are committed to making choices that lead to "Tiena," which means whole health physically, emotionally, spiritually, socially, and financially. As you live day by day, moment by moment, "trusting in Him" instead of your own limited knowledge; you gain access to the enormous "99 percent" wedge of wisdom when you need it.

skip the committee meeting

Now, you may be thinking, *Okay, Dr. Conard. I realize I don't have all the answers, and I am willing to begin living a new way, to gain access to the 99 percent. But I just can't seem to break free from these continual thoughts in my head that are always telling me what to do. The "shoulda, woulda, coulda committee dominates my day, saying things like, "You really should lose weight. You should exercise more. You should drink more water. You should get more sleep," and on and on it goes. I get so tired of it. I don't want to live my life striving to achieve and suffering when I fail. At times, this seems like a worse fate than just doing whatever I want to do and being overweight (or obese). What can I do?*

If this sounds familiar, you are not alone. All of us have experienced this internal tyranny. It is the irritating influence of the "itty-bitty committee." This voice inside our head is a blend of different people from our past, including people like our parents, siblings, teachers, coaches, girlfriends and boyfriends, spouse, bosses, coworkers, children, books, movies, TV, and even ourselves. Every time a problem pops up or we experience something new, the itty-bitty committee wants to share its experiences from the past and tell us what to do. It is always judging and always looking for what is wrong in ourselves, others, and in the situation. It wants us to protect ourselves by reacting defensively and to *decide* on the best course of action based on information from the pages of our past.

Now, there is something interesting about the word *decide*. The suffix *cide* means "to cut off from." Think about some of the words it is used in: insecti*cide*, sui*cide*, geno*cide*, homi*cide*. They all deal with death or the cutting off of life. When we are in a "de*cid*ing" mode with the itty-bitty committee, we are operating in the limited "1 percent" of what *we* know in our mind. In other words, we are leaning on our own understanding and, consequently, disconnected from the "99 percent" wealth of wisdom we don't know. We line up all the possible things we can think of to do from our mind (our past). We then begin to "cut them off" one at a time, thinking, *Nope, not that one, or that one, or that one…* until we are left with the one option that we choose to act on.

In contrast, the Bible says that "the mind of the flesh [which is sense and reason *without* the Holy Spirit] is death…. But the mind of the Spirit is **life** and **peace** [both now and forever]" (Romans 8:6 AMP). So when we rely on the itty-bitty committee and *decide* upon an answer or direction within ourselves, we are doomed to repeat the failures of the past. But if we will turn to what is possible in the 99 percent (to God), we can find the answer.

I have a patient in one of my weight-loss classes who actually coined this phrase *itty-bitty committee*. She has not only learned how to identify its voice but also how to turn a deaf ear to it. She explained that what often happens to her now is, she will find herself in a situation where she is very stressed or anxious or hungry. At that moment when the pressure is on, she will say to herself, *I'm not going to do what I would have done in the past; there is nothing "wrong" here.* She then takes the first healer, which is air, and begins to purposely take some deep breaths. This slows her thinking, reduces the anxiety, and enables her to turn away from the voice of the itty-bitty committee. In this place, she calmly refocuses (re-pents, or re-aims) on her commitment to her life (to her purpose) and chooses to step out in a way that takes her forward, not back into the same old way of acting that got her here in the first place.

Ironically, when I first met her, she didn't have time to work out or relax or change her eating habits. Now that she has learned how to turn from the voice of the committee, she makes better food choices, works out regularly, and takes an hour-long bubble bath before going to bed. She has lost over twenty pounds in about four months and is going strong. She has learned to make the shift from *decisions* to *choices*—from having her past direct her to stepping into her commitments and purpose in life. She is literally *living into her destiny and future.*

David Emerald, in a short book entitled *The Power of TED*, shares how one person was led to make this "shift" from DDT, the "Deadly Drama Triangle," making the same decisions again and again from our past, to TED, The Empowerment Dynamic, choosing new ways and taking "baby steps" toward a new, exciting and empowering future. In the book, he points out the importance of noticing what we are focusing our attention on. If we focus on the problem, anxiety increases and we change what we do for a period of time, until the pressure is off and our anxiety decreases, and then we go back to the old way of acting – a yo-yo of a life that takes us nowhere. In contrast, if we shift and focus on the desired outcome (not how we got there, but what we are committed to achieve), our passion begins to emerge and new baby steps can be taken. A path of continual improvement and growth replaces the cycle of repeating the same past again and again.

Often we find ourselves doing things that we never imagined we would do. The role we play in our lives also shifts. When we are stuck in our past, we experience life as victims of the same old problems or persecutors. We search for something to rescue us from the same old problems and outcomes—the magic pill, or prince charming (who ultimately turns out to have the same issues and problems that previous princes had); it's the same thing, next chapter. *After* we make the shift, we play a much more active role in choosing what to do in our lives. The problem at hand (one of a continual chain of challenges that never stops) becomes the challenge of the day or week to overcome. To successfully create the life we seek, we find time to meditate, listen to music, calm our minds, as well as speak with coaches, consultants, and other people in our lives to help us build new skills and abilities to overcome. We seek to learn a new way of living, not a new way to have a magic solution that will "fix" our lives for us. We turn ourselves over to what life has to offer, not mire in the same old frustrations from our past.

When we begin to tap into this way of living, it becomes clear that this is, in part, what Psalm 32:8 it says, "I will instruct you (says God) and guide you along the best pathway for your life; I will advise you and watch your progress" (TLB). When we nix being a "knower" and become a "learner," we will begin to live our lives on purpose. By living in TED, taking baby steps, leaning into our lives, and not repeating our mistakes, we tap into an amazing source of energy and power. Again in the Old Testament it says,

"Blessed is the man who *trusts in the Lord*, whose confidence is in him. He will be like a tree planted by the water that sends out its roots by the stream. It does not fear when heat comes; its leaves are always green. It has no worries in a year of drought and never fails to bear fruit."
Jeremiah 17:7,8 NIV

The more we stay out of the itty-bitty committee, the more peaceful our heart and mind become and the freer we are to live out our purpose. We are not forced to do something out of fear or guilt. Instead, we are pulled into the possibilities we begin to see in our lives. In the Christian tradition, this is called being led by the Holy Spirit. As a result, we gain access to the wealth of wisdom in the 99 percent that God knows and will send to us as we are open to receive it. This opens doors of new opportunities, new relationships, and new possibilities that we would have never experienced otherwise. Miracles (things that we did not think *could* happen) begin to occur in our lives and the lives of others—things that we never thought or dreamed were possible become possible in this new way of living. We become *transformed*, meaning that we leave our past (the reliance on the itty-bitty committee for guidance) in the past, and we step out into endless possibilities and opportunities.

fan the fire of your heart's desire

So how do we find our purpose? Think back to the years before your "itty-bitty committee" became so strong and overbearing, say when you were in elementary school—the days when you dreamed of what you wanted to be when you grew up. What kind of things got you excited? Was it working with and helping others? Was it being outside and experiencing the wonders of nature? Was it drawing, coloring, and painting pictures? Was it playing with children or caring for animals? Was it solving mysteries or building things with your hands? The things that made you laugh with glee and feel energized about life point toward your purpose.

Now come back to the more recent past. What things bring you lasting joy, peace, love, and fulfillment? In the moments when you experience the greatest satisfaction and pleasure, what activities are you involved in? Writing, singing, acting, cooking, cleaning, or organizing things? Leading a team of people on a special project or doing research on your own? All these things are sign posts that help define your true niche in life.

Once your purpose starts to come into focus, the challenge is then to cut away all the clutter that keeps you from fulfilling it. Sam Walton, the founder of Wal-Mart and Sam's Club, says that the difference between experiencing some success and amazing success is *learning to say no* to anything that takes you away from your purpose. This includes focusing on the failures and pain of the past, the mistakes of the present, and unnecessary weights, like worry and fear, that slow you down and trip you up. When you live in your purpose, you are free to begin asking yourself in each situation you face, *What would a person with my purpose and destiny do in this situation?* With this clarity, our lives begin to move faster and become freer. As a good friend of mine, Venus Opal-Reece, teaches in her course Street Smarts: From Surviving to Thriving, it is at this point that we become uncluttered and begin to appreciate great *velocity* in our lives.

live your destiny!

Perhaps one of the best ways to help you capture the essence of your purpose is to ask one thought-provoking question: If you could write your own eulogy, what would it be? In other words, what kind of things do you want people to say about you when you die—how would you want to be remembered?

We are gathered together today to celebrate the life of _____
_____.

To me, he/she was the embodiment of _____.

I could always count on him/her to _____.

I will never forget when he/she did_____.

My life would not have been the same if I had not known him/her.

Don't rush to answer. Quietly ponder the thought, and then listen for the reply that arises in your heart. The answer to this question paints a vivid picture of who you really want to be. This is the essence of your purpose.

Why go through this effort? Why define your purpose? To the degree that you identify and utilize your gifts and strengths is the degree to which you are going to have peace, love, joy, patience, kindness, self-control, and fulfillment in your life. I encourage you to surrender your itty-bitty committee and tap into the limitless joys of living your life this new way. This shift makes all the difference. It moves us from having been alive, to really living. Mark Batterson articulates this:

> **"Quit living as if the purpose of life is to arrive safely at death… Expand your horizons… Blaze new trails… Go after a dream that is destined to fail without divine intervention."[2]**

Be willing to fail and forgive yourself as opposed to trying not to fail. Seek to discover your purpose, acknowledge the Creator of the 99 percent and be open to huge, amazing, miraculous possibilities in your life. Life is meant to be lived in action, not thought about in "committee." It is my most sincere wish for you that you will begin to thrive with velocity in your life on purpose.

A QUICK ENCAPSULATION

Purpose is Healer #7. Having purpose is having a reason for living—it is the "why" behind what we do. Without it, we have no direction, no meaning, no fulfillment. You have a unique destiny. Discovering your purpose begins with and finds full expression in letting go of being a "knower" and embracing a new way of living as a "learner"—living not in the 1 percent that you know but in the 99 percent that you don't know. It is in this that you will find the joy and fulfillment that you seek. As you trust with all your heart and lean not on your own understanding, your path of purpose will emerge and become clear.

LOCATE YOURSELF

Locate your purpose by asking yourself some simple questions like…

- What did I dream of doing as child—what did I consistently aspire to be when I grew up?
- What am I naturally good at—sports, music, research, solving problems, public speaking, building things?
- What do I enjoy doing? What past jobs, hobbies, ministries, etc., gave me a real sense of joy, peace, and fulfillment?
- Which do I like using most: my hands, my mind, or my mouth?
- How is my personality? Am I a behind-the-scenes person or do I like a lot of attention? Do I like to be in charge, or would I rather follow someone else's leading?

- If I could do anything at all—*anything*—and I knew I wouldn't fail, what would I do?
- If education, money, health, age and time were not obstacles, what would I pursue?

Answer these questions honestly and jot down your responses in a journal or notebook. Do you see some common ground between them? They are pointing the way to your individual purpose.

YOUR SEVEN HEALERS SCORE

Rate yourself on a 1 – 10 scale: 1 – Never, 3 – Sometimes, 5 – Half the time, 7 – Mostly, and 10 – Always, on these statements;

_____ I am living a life of freedom and peace.

_____ I am grateful for all that I have been given in life.

_____ I am managing the things I control, encouraging those I influence, and trusting things will work out with the things I don't control.

Recommended Resources: *The Power of TED*, David Emerald (Polaris Publishing WA, 2009) *Wild Goose Chase*, Mark Batterson (Colorado Springs, CO, Multnomah Books, 2008).

(1) Wild Goose Chase, Mark Batterson (Colorado Springs, CO, Multnomah Books, 2008) pp. 16-17. (2) See note 1, pp. 171-173.

conclusion
MY AWAKENING

As you come to the end of this book, hopefully, you are coming to the beginning of viewing the possibility of a whole new way of living. I don't know exactly where you are in your life, but I want to encourage you not to feel hopeless! This way of living life is a game changer, a getting out of your mind (the 1 percent) and into what is possible (the 99 percent). It will end the suffering in your life and give you a free walk into an empowered, light, exciting, thrilling experience. Trust me...I am speaking from experience.

life was a mess

There was a time in my life many years ago when I felt hopeless and miserable. I was operating my medical practice and seeing patients, but I was basically just going through the motions. I had reached a point in my career where I disliked being a physician. I worked harder and harder but experienced less and less gratification and satisfaction. The hours were long, and the malpractice threat was oppressive. My insurance and other costs kept going up. I worked more hours to earn the same amount every year. In addition, my patients didn't seem to understand the importance of my medical advice. I explained what they needed to do to manage their diabetes, high cholesterol, hypertension, etc. But they didn't seem to hear me. They kept doing the same things they had done before, gaining weight, requiring higher doses of medicine, complaining about their medical and medication bills. I felt I was merely babysitting them on their way to the grave. I was discouraged.

I was experiencing a major crisis in my life. I felt trapped. I often overslept. When I went to work, I didn't want to be there. I became cynical, angry, frustrated, aggravated, and irritated. I was not a pleasant person to work with. I alienated myself from just about every person I was in a relationship with. I was out of touch with my purpose for living.

At this time in my life, I was overweight and out of shape. I weighed about 242 pounds and did not exercise. I was prediabetic, my good cholesterol was down, and my bad cholesterol was up (and climbing). Ironically, when I looked in the mirror I was a perfect reflection of what I was complaining about in my patients. Moreover, these health problems were merely a byproduct and reflection of how I viewed my life—I saw myself as the victim, living at the mercy of my life, frustrated and miserable. I was so busy, but I was burning the candle at both ends. I felt tremendous fatigue. I became quite lonely. The way I was living was totally incompatible with the concepts of the Seven Healers.

My family life suffered, and my wife and I separated. This was the wake-up call that eventually brought me to my senses. I became a tightly-wound ball of anger and frustration that was gradually losing control. I blamed others rather than myself. My life revolved around external signs of success. I became a man seeking the approval of others—focused on material possessions, prestige, and self-gain.

a life or death struggle

One night when I was at home alone, something happened to me that became a major turning point in my life. As I sat and pondered my situation, I suddenly felt as if I had been hit by lightning—BOOM—and was falling backwards in my chair. Instantly, a statement shot into my head—so strong it seemed like an audible voice. I heard the words, *You must die.*

Over the next few months, as if in a bad nightmare, I ruminated on this thought. I considered the idea that I might be better off if I were to kill myself. I had a large life insurance policy, but in order for my family to collect on it, my death would have to look like an accident. In my thoughts I actually began to think of ways I could commit suicide and make it look like an accident. Then, out of nowhere came the strong conviction, *But I don't want to die!*

I don't know where these voices came from—my mind, my spirit, or the Holy Spirit. What an internal tug-of-war that was. What should I do? The thought of going to sleep and just not waking up sounded perfect; if I could just figure out how to have it happen naturally. But I knew down deep that this was not going to happen. Another idea entered my consciousness, "I can 'die' to who I am, without my body dying." About two or three weeks after this happened, I humbled myself and spoke to my wife. I said to her, "I need to die to who I am, but I don't know what to do."

She said she understood and, to my surprise and relief, she was committed to our relationship. As she recommended, I began going to a local church with her in our community. I was probably difficult to be around: one day meek and easy-going and the next wound up and angry. I was still caught in my victim mentality.

Gradually, slowly (over years) my "addiction" to my thoughts passed, and I understood that my thoughts were incomplete, limited, and often a misguided conclusion: They were not the "truth." I began taking responsibility for my actions—I began to create the life I wanted to live. I determined I would stay in my commitments to all others in my life. I would be open to new possibilities and trust this new way to lead and guide me in every area of my life. I rebuilt my relationship with my wife. Finally, my life was headed in a better direction.

As the saying goes, "How you do anything is how you do everything." I began to appreciate and discover the principles of the Seven Healers, incorporating them into my life and my practice. In 2000 a medical healer named Brazos Minshew, a naturopathic doctor, brought more clarity and understanding to the Seven Healers. We discussed and explored their role considerably. I came alive inside when I realized, This has the possibility of helping everybody! I became so excited about these principles for living that when the new practice, TienaHealth, opened, I invited Dr. Minshew to join me. He did and together we continued to develop the concepts of the Seven Healers.

my greatest desire for you

Fourteen years have passed since my awakening. Now, I love my job and the people I work with. I can hardly wait to get up in the morning and go to work. I truly love my patients and I am getting along very well with the people in my life. Oddly enough, I am going to the same practice, treating many of the same patients, and receiving the same compensation. This is a miracle that occurred in my life by making the shift away from seeing myself as a "victim" and living inside the 1 percent. I am now liberated from my old way of thinking and am free to experience the possibilities of the 99 percent. I feel transformed physically, emotionally, spiritually, socially and financially. I feel free to experience a complete and blessed life. In the Bible, it says,

"God can do anything, you know—far more than you could ever imagine or guess or request in your wildest dreams! He does it not by pushing us around but by working within us, his Spirit deeply and gently within us."
Ephesians 3:20[2]

My greatest desire for you is that this book will help you in your journey. Instead of it taking you years, as it did me, I pray you are able to understand these principles and put them into practice in a matter of months, weeks, or even days!

Regardless of where you wish to end your journey, begin by incorporating the Seven Healers in your life every day. Become aware of your use of *Air*, taking regular deep breaths and practicing deep-breathing exercises to calm your mind and body. Take in adequate *Water* and keep yourself hydrated. Aim at getting 54 hours of *Sleep* a week, and your body will thank you for it. Take in the best medicine for the body by choosing fresh fruits and vegetables, lean meats and whole-grain *Food*, and manage the quantity by using the Hand Signals of Health. Take in the best medicine for the body and *Play* for 30 minutes, 5 days/week. Nurture strong, healthy *Relationships* with people who are willing to hold you accountable and who will support and encourage you as you discover and live your life on *Purpose*.

It is my humble wish that you will find and maintain a life of joy and peace, living with favor and experiencing the miracles life has to offer.

(1) Christian Quotes on Relationship with God (http://dailychristianquote.com/dcqrelationshipgod.html, retrieved 3/23/10). (2) Scripture taken from The Message.

calculate your seven healers score

Rate yourself on a 1 – 10 scale: 1 – Never, 3 – Sometimes, 5 – Half the time, 7 – Mostly, and 10 – Always, on these statements;

RAPHA ONE : AIR

_____ I am aware of my body and take deep breathes to manage my stress.
_____ I put aside time to practice deep breathing (progressive relaxation).

RAPHA TWO : WATER

_____ I reach my water-drinking goal every day (enough water to make my "water" clear or light yellow.)
_____ I substitute water for sugared and/or caffeinated beverages.

RAPHA THREE : SLEEP

_____ I sleep 54 hours each week.
_____ I am consistent with the time of night that I go to sleep and/or the time of morning that I wake up.

RAPHA FOUR : FOOD

_____ I use the hand Signals of Health when I eat.
_____ I eat a rainbow of vegetables and fruits at the first part of my meals each day.
_____ I am a success in reducing saturated fat, trans fats, refined carbohydrates, high fructose corn syrup and sugar.
_____ I successfully add monounsaturated fats and deep water fish (or fish oil supplements) to my diet.
_____ I eat balanced meals and snacks (protein, carbohydrate, and fat).

RAPHA FIVE : PLAY

_____ I am active and play for at least 150 minutes per week or over 6000 steps/day.

_____ I incorporate resistance training, aerobic activity, and flexibility exercises into my exercise program.

RAPHA SIX : RELATIONSHIPS

_____ I spend time with friends who call me to be my best and encourage me in my life.

_____ I give without expectation to the people I come in contact with.

_____ I forgive myself and others for things that don't go well.

RAPHA SEVEN : PURPOSE

_____ I am living a life of freedom and peace.

_____ I am grateful for all that I have been given in life.

_____ I am managing the things I control, encouraging those I influence, and trusting things will work out with the things I don't control.

_____TOTAL SCORE

YOUR SEVEN HEALERS SCORE:

- If your score is < 50 your lifestyle does not currently support healthy living,
- If you are 50 – 80 you may have some significant issues,
- 80 – 120 you are on your way to health!
- >120 you are on your way to a great life!

www.rapha7ven.com

THE SEVEN HEALERS

SIMPLE BUT POWERFUL WISDOM FOR AN EXTRAORDINARY LIFE

BOOK · AUDIOBOOK CD · DIGITAL MP3

Dr. Conard's passion is to help people live longer and better lives. A national expert on disease prevention, Scott is reaching out to the many Americans who are worried about their health, are concerned about their weight, and are frustrated because prior diets and exercise plans have fallen short. He believes going to a health care provider should be an entertaining and educational "wow" experience.

Scott's father and role model is also a family practice doctor. His day-to-day passion to help people in Bradenton, Florida inspired Scott to continue the family tradition.

The most rewarding part of Scott's job is helping people improve the quality of their life by discovering for themselves improved health. He is an advocate for empowering people to take control of their health. Scott genuinely believes in his patients and is dedicated to sharing concepts that will change their lives.

Dr. Conard is the founder of the TienaHealth Medical Group and maintains his private practice as Medical Director for Tiena Health and also serves as Chief Medical Officer of Medical Edge Healthcare Group, PA. Scott lives in Southlake, Texas, with his wife and four children and enjoys singing, public speaking, exercise, traveling and photography.